1000 TOP TIPS
for **MUMS** & **DADS**

1000 TOP TIPS

for MUMS & DADS

How to keep your kids healthy, safe and smiling

Peggy Vance

DUNCAN BAIRD PUBLISHERS

LONDON

1000 Top Tips for Mums & Dads
Peggy Vance

To Sky, Biba and Jas Kang; and in memory of Leila Jane Thompson

First published in the United Kingdom and Ireland in 2006 by
Duncan Baird Publishers Ltd
Sixth Floor
Castle House
75–76 Wells Street
London W1T 3QH

Created and designed by Duncan Baird Publishers

Managing Editor: Ingrid Court-Jones
Editor: Adam Parfitt
Managing Designer: Dan Sturges
Designer: Sailesh Patel
Commissioned artwork: Natacha Ledwidge

British Library Cataloguing-in-Publication Data:
A CIP record for this book is available from the British Library

ISBN-10: 1-84483-228-7   ISBN-13: 9-781844-832286

10 9 8 7 6 5 4 3 2 1

Typeset in AT Shannon
Colour reproduction by Colourscan, Singapore
Printed in Thailand by Imago

PUBLISHER'S NOTE
While every care has been taken to ensure that the advice offered in this book is
sound and safe, no responsibility can be taken by the author or the publishers for
any loss, damage or injury caused by reliance on the information contained herein.

Contents

Introduction

I've been a parent for over a decade, but I'm still learning new tricks. In fact, I have lots of ideas today – my own and those gleaned from other people – that it would have been really useful to have known years ago.

1000 Top Tips for Mums and Dads is intended to save you from having to wait until situations arise before thinking up ways and means of tackling them. Of course, every parent will find their own way of doing things, but some tricks of the trade are so useful that it's easier to be spoon-fed them from the outset.

You may find some of the tips in this book more useful than others – there's absolutely no reason why you shouldn't pick and choose between them: "That's not right for us, but this is." "It's a good idea, but I'll adapt it." "I'd never thought of that; let's try it out."

Thankfully, I haven't had to come up with a thousand tips all on my own. Friends, family, health professionals and parents far and wide have offered invaluable snippets of advice that they'd like to pass on to others. As a result, this book is a sort of database of parents' wisdom, covering many different aspects of the biggest (and best) job in the world – being a mum or a dad. Organized into various thematic sections, it offers tips on everything from practical matters in early infancy to handing the emotions of older kids. You'll also find lots of wacky and creative ideas that encourage you to make the most of your time with your children. Some may seem completely off the wall, others more conventional. There's something here for everyone, and each family will be able to take from this book thoughts and suggestions that will make a difference to their daily lives.

There's a lot here, too, to help you tackle the daily challenge of keeping your children safe and healthy. Every parent will have the odd mishap (I remember my son falling out of his buggy when I hadn't secured the straps to go just a few yards up the road!), but all the better if these can be anticipated and avoided. New mums and dads will, hopefully, find *1000 Top Tips for Mums and Dads* particularly useful for this reason, but it's amazing how even more experienced parents can find that they haven't considered something that, on reflection, makes perfect sense.

So, enjoy! Take what you want; leave what you don't want; and have a fun, safe and happy time with your children.

Chapter 1
The Developing Child

Babies and toddlers

Learn about breastfeeding while you are pregnant. If possible, get advice and tips from recent mothers and, if you go to an antenatal group, ask questions so as to prepare yourself to give breastfeeding your best shot.

Don't be put off breastfeeding by well-meaning people who tell you that you will be drained of energy, have no time to yourself and have your freedom severely limited. Although there is a grain of truth in these arguments, the bottom line is that breast milk is the ideal foodstuff for your baby, it helps get your body back to its pre-pregnant state and it is free, portable and always available.

Know that breast is best. Unless there is a good reason to use formula, stick with breast milk. Even a month of exclusive breastfeeding will benefit your child's immune system, brain development and long-term health. Mixed feeding, where breast milk is supplemented by formula, should be delayed for as long as possible, particularly when babies are born into a family with a history of eczema, asthma or hay fever. If you feel that breastfeeding isn't working for you, consult your doctor, midwife or health visitor before you stop: they may be able to offer you the support and backup you need.

Steer clear of eating citrus fruits and curry, and avoid caffeine and other stimulants if your breastfeeding baby is unusually wakeful or colicky.

Lean back to breastfeed if you feel your milk is coming out too quickly for your baby to swallow comfortably.

Don't be afraid to breastfeed in public. Breasts are meant for breastfeeding, so breastfeed however and wherever you like – within reason. But note that restaurants in some countries can ban breastfeeding on their premises by law, so it's best to ask first so that you can go elsewhere if they do not allow it.

Wear a practical top for breastfeeding – either a loose-fitting one that can be lifted up or a nursing top with openings for feeding. Button-up tops and shirts that you have to open down the middle tend to be much more revealing.

Buy a breast pump only if you know it's a really good one. Using a poorly designed hand pump can be very demoralizing. Ask friends and family members for their recommendations and talk to your health visitor or contact a breastfeeding support organization to see which makes and models they suggest. Many women find that they have greater success with an electric pump. These are pricey, but can often be hired.

Start to express milk while your baby is still a few weeks old and gradually introduce the occasional feed in a bottle. Older babies, who are already well used to the breast, can be very resistant to accepting breast milk from a bottle. Expressing as much milk as possible gives you some freedom and allows your partner to spend more one-to-one time with the baby, including the odd night shift!

Lie on your side to feed, with your baby tucked under your lower arm. This position is great when you are tired and don't want the weight of the baby in your arms. It also gives your breasts a rest from the pull of gravity and the downward sucking action.

Have a breast code. It's best to alternate feeds between breasts but very easy to lose track of which breast should be next. Lots of women devise their own aide-mémoires, such as changing a safety pin from one bra strap to the other or – simpler still – transferring a bangle between wrists.

Abandon complicated cooking when you have a newborn. If family or friends ask what you'd like, suggest that they bring you a care package of homemade ready meals, cold meats, pre-prepared salads and other instant foodstuffs.

Limit visitors to your new baby, ideally to immediate family only. If you can't avoid seeing a lot of people, group visitors |into one part of the day so that for the majority of the time you can rest, relax and recuperate.

Look at each other. Your new baby can't focus beyond around 12in (30cm), which is about the distance from your breast to your face. Stay close when playing or chatting so as to have eye contact.

Banish flowers from around a newborn baby. The infant is just getting used to breathing and can well do without the air being heavy with pollen, a well-known allergen. In advance of the birth, tactfully tell friends that, if they want to buy something, a little gift for the baby would be preferred ... nappies are always useful!

Don't wear perfume. Young babies have enough to cope with in their new environment without having to inhale scent. Go easy on all pungent toiletries until your young one's respiratory system is more mature. Be particularly careful not to spray aerosol hairsprays or deodorants near your baby, and the same goes for air fresheners.

Don't overcommit yourself in the weeks before and after the birth. Give your growing family the time and space to take things easy.

Accept mood swings. After the birth, the mother's hormones go into free fall. Being emotional is a feature of the first few days with a new baby, and many mums feel guilty and confused to be sobbing over their newborn child. Treat having a cry as you would having a laugh: let your feelings out, let them run their course, then let them pass.

Crying checklist

If your baby is crying, run through a mental checklist of what might be the cause:

- **Hungry?**
- **Tired?**
- **Wet or dirty?**
- **Hot or cold?**
- **Uncomfortable?**
- **Bored?**
- **In pain?**
- **Ill?**

Keep a packed changing bag at the front door so that you can go out with the baby at short notice. Bags that are like big sacks aren't ideal as you have to rummage about in them every time you change your baby. Rather, choose bags with compartments – ideally with see-through pockets, like make-up artists' bags – so that what you need is readily to hand.

Have a pop-up cot for travels and visits. A pop-up cot is small, like a carrycot. Made of flimsy nylon on a wire frame, it twists flat, then literally pops into three dimensions when taken out of its bag. If you take it with you when you are out and about, you can settle your baby down almost anywhere for a comfortable, flat-on-the-back sleep.

Have baby "stops". In each of the rooms you use most frequently, have a soft, safe place where you can lie or sit your baby down out of harm's way.

Make a soft nest around a wobbly baby who's just learning to sit up. Pack pillows, quilts and the like snugly around their bottom so that any tumbles will be cushioned. Stick around to avert any danger of smothering.

Massage your baby. Fretful babies can be soothed and calmed by gentle caresses. Lie your baby on a soft surface in a quiet, warm room. Gently, using a little olive or baby oil, smooth your hands along the length of their arms, legs and back, stroking their skin as if stroking a cat. Avoid any vigorous massage movements.

Ask for what you need. If people enquire what you would like for your new baby, do make suggestions. If you don't, you are likely to end up with dozens of Babygros and not a lot else!

Buy neutral colours. If all the clothes for your baby are in gender-specific colours and styles, you won't be able to reuse them if your next child is of a different sex. Opt for gender neutrals such as green, yellow, red, orange, brown, cream and white.

Don't dress to impress. Babies and toddlers look cute in dresses, but they can be highly impractical. Babies get them in a twist, crawlers kneel on them, cruisers trip on them and toddlers catch them on things. Put one on, take a photograph, then take it off again!

Choose bibs with sleeves for babies who tend to play with their food.

Prioritize poppers. When buying clothes for your baby, value comfort and convenience over style and tradition. Buy vest "bodies" that pop-fasten at the crotch so they don't ride up, and trousers with pop-open legs for easy changing.

Provide activity toys. Choose colourful, textural and noisy toys for young babies. The more the toy does, and the easier it is for babies to handle, the more they'll engage with it. Simple, old-fashioned rattles that can be grabbed and banged are firm favourites. Soft toys mean nothing to babies!

Play copycats. Stick your tongue out and your young baby may well try to copy you. Put your face close to theirs and entertain them with a facial mime show. Make noises, open and shut your mouth and grin at your baby. Observe what they do in response.

Stimulate your baby. Go out together, have people around, lie your baby where it's possible to see what's going on and encourage other children to play with them. Babies thrive on activity and are usually far less grizzly if entertained.

Allow noise. A baby should be able to sleep through noise, so allow a reasonable hubbub in the house. Babies like to know that they are near to people and haven't been abandoned!

Make a mobile out of objects that will attract your baby's attention, in bright colours, with strong tonal contrasts. Suspend these from a frame made of a couple of coat hangers joined at right angles, and keep the mobile well out of baby's reach.

Use baby books with babies of all ages, including newborns. Start with cloth or board books containing vibrant patterns that your baby will find interesting. Prop the books open around where your baby is lying so that they can gaze at them.

Use toys at changing time. From about four months old babies can get tremendously wriggly during changes. Distract your infant by putting a baby-gym frame over the changing mat so that they can play and give you vital seconds in which to change the nappy.

Stay in the swim of things. Even though you've had a new baby, it's still possible to stay in touch with the outside world. Put on the radio, watch a bit of TV, scan the newspapers and chat to friends on the phone. You'll get interrupted, but you'll still feel better for it.

Share your baby. Let your baby be held by other people. Babies who get liberally passed around tend to be less clingy and more at ease when looked after by others. Moreover, if other people take a turn, you can take a break.

Position the buggy so that, when stationary, it has its back to the sun or oncoming wind, is as far as possible from exhaust emissions and gives the baby or toddler a reasonable view of what is going on.

Position car seats and bouncing chairs on the floor where there's no danger of them falling off a high surface if they shift with the baby's movement.

Treasure little tootsies. Babies' bones are soft and malleable so should not be restricted by footwear. Moreover, there are masses of balance receptors in the soles of the feet. When learning to walk, a child should ideally be barefoot, although this is not always practical. Until your baby is walking unaided, let them wear soft baby socks or booties that have ample space around the toes. First shoes must be fitted properly and only worn outdoors. When your child is inside, revert to socks and booties.

Chat away to your baby. Whatever you are doing – nappy changing, going round the shops, tackling chores – tell your baby what's going on. And if you are reading while breastfeeding, why not read aloud? The intonation of your voice and your speech patterns will be fascinating to your young baby.

Sleep when the baby sleeps. Even if there seem to be a million things to do during that precious time when your baby doesn't need you, force yourself – even if only once a day – to have a snooze with your baby.

Buy a Bumbo, a squashy, wipe-clean seat that hugs your baby's back, bottom and legs to support them comfortably and securely in an upright position. Suitable for use from four months, this is perfect for mealtimes.

Open a bank account for your new baby into which, throughout their childhood, you can deposit monetary gifts from family and friends. Kids' accounts offer tax-efficient saving, but it's still worth shopping around to compare rates and offers from providers.

Tackle accidents on the carpet by blotting with cloths. Dab the stain with detergent solution, blot it again, then dab it with a solution of one-third vinegar, two-thirds water. Rinse it and blot it once more.

Don't be surprised! All little boys fiddle with their willies. Gone (thank goodness) are the days when outraged parents punished this terrible "sin". But there's nothing wrong with telling children not to fiddle in company, just as you might tell them not to eat with their mouths open or not to wipe their noses on their sleeves.

Keep toddlers close when you go out to eat. Kids crawling underfoot and waiters with trays of hot food and drinks make a poor combination.

Rein them in. Two-year-olds don't think leading reins are demeaning! If a toddler is an uncertain walker, or likely to wander off or run away, they are essential. Choose harness-style reins rather than a wrist strap, as these are more comfortable and offer better security against falls.

Take heart. Having a new baby is an emotional challenge for both parents. Accept that you may not get on with your partner perfectly all the time, and try to take the occasional spat in your stride.

Young children

Turn a deaf ear. Little children are fascinated and vastly entertained by anything to do with bottoms: poo, wee and willies are a hot topic of infant conversation. Most children go through this phase, so unless it gets completely out of hand, just pretend you haven't heard what they are saying to each other!

Keep a funny book. From the moment they start to speak, get a big blank book in which to write down all the wonderful things your kids say. In later years this book will be a treasured family keepsake and will give you and your children a big laugh!

Do daft things. Young children love it when adults do crazy and unusual things, and they really enjoy strange and bizarre events. Satisfy this love of the surreal with some zany fun. You might, for instance, make up a game like Banana Bag (squashing a banana inside a thick, clear plastic bag!), Pass the Eyeball (asking them to close their eyes and handing round a peeled grape) or Wobbly Stool (lying back and letting your children ride on your raised knees, which you wobble and then unexpectedly collapse). Make the most of these games – they give you visiting rights to your child's world.

Point out differences between things, such as different sorts of dogs, types of shops, varying landscapes or contrasting flowers, so that your young children start to observe and become interested in the diversity of the world around them.

Explore the senses. Make connections between different sensual experiences: sight, sound, taste, smell and touch. "What colour do you think this music is?" "What sound would a banana make?" "What do you reckon blue smells of?" Where older children might think you mad, younger ones are far more likely to accept such associations and try to offer answers.

Make associations between people and colours, sounds, shapes, fruits, drinks, landscapes ... anything! Sometimes be the interviewer – "What sort of animal are you?" "What sort of shape are you?" – and at other times the interviewee. Older children will enjoy finding associations for all their friends, and then quizzing those friends to see if the associations tally.

Use metaphors and similes. The capacity to make connections between things is the basis of imagination, so share with your kids any associations that occur to you: "Those parachutes look like jellyfish in the sky." "The water coming out of the tap looks plaited, just like your hair is now." "Look at your shadow – you're a giant statue!"

Work out the meaning of what your kids say. Young children's speech can be very disjointed. Often kids burble on about seemingly unconnected things and it's all too easy not to hear. If you do listen really hard, you'll be surprised by how much sense can be construed from the kaleidoscope of infant speech.

Quash pester power. If all else fails, steer clear of pester hot spots. Choose the supermarket that doesn't sell toys over the one that does, take a different route to avoid the sweet shop or leave your partner to babysit while you shop alone in the evenings. What the eye doesn't see, the infant doesn't hanker for.

Avert tantrums with distractions: "Look at those lovely flowers!" "I think I saw Poppy the cat outside the window!" "Can you spot a red car?" "What would you like for your birthday?" It doesn't always work, but it's worth a go!

Bin flip-flops. They look cute on young kids but are very difficult for children to run about and tackle stairs in. Properly fitted sandals, with backs, are infinitely preferable, and far safer.

Insist upon plates. Young children can be fantastically messy eaters. From an early age, train them not to wander about while eating, to eat over a plate or surface and to be mindful of how much mess they are making.

Dress the part. Left to their own devices, most younger children would ice-skate in swimming costumes and play tennis in winter coats – without noticing. Dressing appropriately is not high on a kid's list of priorities, so lay down the law.

Move on. Young children develop very fast. A toy that was fascinating a month ago may be of little interest now, so keep abreast of your child's curiosity and developing intellect by presenting them with fresh challenges and activities. You needn't spend a fortune – toy libraries, charity shops and imaginative activities won't break the bank.

Older children

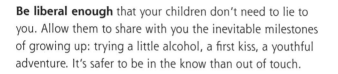

Give your advice, not your opinion.

Answer their questions about sex straightforwardly and candidly, without offering more information than you think they need to know at their age and stage.

Be liberal enough that your children don't need to lie to you. Allow them to share with you the inevitable milestones of growing up: trying a little alcohol, a first kiss, a youthful adventure. It's safer to be in the know than out of touch.

Don't jump to conclusions. If you disapprove of something your child does, try not to aggrandize it with your outrage. One drink does not make an alcoholic, nor one cigarette a smoker. Better to have a mature discussion about health than a slanging match about your fears for the future.

Allow freedom of expression in fashion, music, interests and pastimes. So long as your bottom lines are met – your children must be safe, kind and conscientious! – cut them a bit of slack around the things that matter to them but don't have to matter to you.

Respect privacy. Let older children open their own post, have private telephone conversations and close the door when they have friends over to play. A respect for your child's privacy is unlikely to compromise their safety.

Offer wall space. If you have a newly decorated house, put up pinboards in your children's bedrooms so they can customize a bit of wall without getting into trouble! Use brightly coloured map pins that are easy to spot if they fall out.

Have secret signals. If public displays of affection embarrass your child, develop your own code – it could be a low five for a kiss and a high five for a hug, or a pat on the shoulder for a kiss and a gentle punch on the arm for a hug. Big kids need affection, but are much more likely to accept it on their own terms.

Baby your older children when they need it and there's no one else around to make them feel self-conscious. Tuck them into bed, cuddle them, stroke their hair and whisper your love to them. Soothe away cares just as you did when they were little.

Teach baby care, for two main reasons: so as to bring up useful and responsible young adults who could safely babysit, and – even more importantly – to demonstrate the never-ending work involved in caring for an infant.

Don't pry into your children's lives. Kids love to keep a secret diary or a box of treasured possessions that they can lock, so let them do so – unless of course you need to know for serious reasons of health or safety, such as if you suspect that they could be taking drugs.

Pre-school childcare

Childminder/nanny checklist

Here are some questions to ask a potential childcare provider:

- **Do you have any childcare qualifications?**
- **Do you have any First Aid qualifications?**
- **What is your experience with children?**
- **Have you previously looked after children of a similar age?**
- **Do you have any references?**
- **Can you cook?**
- **What would you cook in a typical week?**
- **What activities will you undertake with the children?**
- **When and where would you take them out?**
- **When are you available/unavailable?**
- **Have you any dependants/family commitments that might affect your work?**

Allow settling-in time. With any new childcare provider or nursery, give your child a chance to familiarize themselves with the new faces and surroundings, ideally over a few days before they start. Later, judge for yourself whether a swift or drawn out goodbye makes the separation less painful for your child.

Don't be intimidated by "nursery policy" or opinionated staff. Leaving your child for the first time is an emotional business and you need to do it in a way that feels right for both you and your little one.

Ask carers for the low-down on your child's day – it's useful to know roughly when they slept and what they ate so you don't feed them the same again at home or try to put them to bed before they are tired.

Brief the babysitter. Try to let your kids meet the sitter before the evening of your absence so as to gauge how well they'll get on. Agree a fee and hours in advance, and leave full contact details. Show and demonstrate where things are and how you want things done, rather than just talking them through, and do as much dinner/bedtime preparation as you can before leaving the house. Call to say if you'll be late (ask them to answer the phone!), pay in full for any overtime and always arrange for them to get home safely.

School

Explore the choices of available schools, however limited they may seem. Check out the school's prospectus and website, read its latest report from the educational inspectorate, consider its exam results (if these are published) and – most importantly – find out what pupils and their parents think of it. Ask to tour the school on an open day or make a personal appointment to be shown around. Write a list of what's important to you in a school to double-check that what you've seen (however impressive) matches up to what you want.

Explain the difference between parents and teachers. Make sure your child understands that it is your job to show them how to behave properly and the teachers' to tell them about interesting things. Make it clear that the teachers shouldn't have to do your job!

Take a photo on the morning of the first day at school. Not only will it become a treasured piece of family history, but in making your child feel proud and special it will help them to square up to the challenges ahead.

Leave plenty of time to get to school, especially in the early days. A child who is harried first thing in the morning will be more easily rattled throughout the day than one who's had time to get their bearings. You will also feel better for not having to nag and chivvy. Sacrifice 10 minutes' sleep for the sake of a peaceful start.

Read the syllabus your child is following, so that you know what the teachers are trying to get across. You might also want to plan trips and visits that complement your child's areas of study.

Take a look through school exercise books and judge for yourself the strengths and weaknesses of your child's written work.

Don't wait for parents' evening. If there's something you're worried about, make an appointment to see your child's teacher. If you have a criticism, tread gently and try to put yourself in the teacher's shoes before you say anything you'll regret. Try to maintain a constructive and balanced dialogue while sorting out any problems.

Identify and address special needs. If you suspect that your child may have special educational needs – whether in being gifted, in having a condition such as dyslexia or dyspraxia, or in needing specific educational support – discuss your concerns with the child's school and request that an assessment is made. If special needs are identified, it is reasonable to expect the school to put forward proposals to address those needs.

Deal promptly with any paperwork to do with your child's school. All too often parents are asked to respond immediately or else miss a great opportunity or event. Your kids may not mind if you don't show up to a parents' evening, but they are likely to be broken-hearted if they miss a school trip because you didn't return the consent form. It's worth searching their pockets and schoolbags for forgotten circulars, too.

Offer praise where it's due. Don't keep your appreciation to yourself. Let your child's teacher know if you think they are doing a particularly good job or if a topic of study or a school trip has gone well. We all need praise – and it will take the sting out of any criticisms you may later have to voice!

Make friends with the teachers but keep enough distance to allow you still to be able to raise issues and concerns.

Join in! Do what you can to participate and contribute to the school community. Even if you are busy working, try to take on the odd responsibility. Show your children that their school is important to you.

Live a little! If you've been busy at work and then need to do something with the children – maybe attend school speech day or a parents' evening – treat it like a mini-holiday together. Stop for coffee, take in a movie in the early evening or go out to the park for some ball games. Try to wring maximum fun out of any extra spare time you get with your kids.

Show up. Even if your child is only competing in the egg and spoon race, try to get to school sports day. If they are merely a sheep in the school Nativity play, make sure you're in the audience. Demonstrate that their contribution – however small – gives you pleasure and makes you proud.

Judge your contribution. It's fine to be vocal in supporting your kids on the school field, but judge what you shout and how loudly you shout it! Hollering throughout the game can be distracting for the other players and excruciatingly embarrassing for your child.

Button your lip. Whatever your thoughts about your children's teachers, keep your judgments low-key. Neither your kids' behaviour nor the quality of the teaching will improve if there's a loss of respect.

Remember which class your child is in! Take on board your kids' details. If you don't, you may show yourself up and hurt their feelings. Strive to recall things that are important in their world.

Don't let your kids stay off school because they haven't finished their homework, or because they're tired or (unless unavoidable) because a sibling is off school. If you allow absence for petty reasons, getting your child to school can become a daily negotiation.

Keep track. If your child has a school homework diary, ask them to write out fully and legibly what it is they have to do. If all they've written is "Do sheet", it can be very difficult to help! Also, writing out the task properly makes them concentrate on what is being set. Check the diary each night and sign it if necessary.

Stress the importance of good presentation. No teacher – or examiner – enjoys marking messy or scrappy work. Check that your children are taking reasonable care to turn in work that's as neat as they can manage.

Don't pile on the pressure. Some of the greatest figures in modern world history have shown little ability in school. So long as you feel your kids are making an effort to do their best and that you are supporting their learning, try to be content with whatever they achieve.

Cultivate confidence. School should leave your child's self-esteem intact. Talk to the teacher if you think that it is under threat from any quarter, be it from other children, teachers or the pace or nature of the work.

Think before you quiz. Don't always ask the same questions when your children come out of school, or you'll get the same answers and learn almost nothing new.

Teach pencil-case management. Make it the responsibility of your child to check that the appropriate equipment – in working order – is in their pencil case throughout the school term.

Choose your child's schoolbag with care. If you have a choice, go for a backpack-style bag of semi-rigid construction with a well-padded back and straps. These are much easier to pack and unpack, keep schoolbooks in better condition than sack-style bags and are designed to spread the load evenly to avoid back strain. Look out for backpacks specifically approved by back pain organizations.

Don't risk it. Advise your kids only to take to school or lend to other children possessions that they can bear to lose.

Extra-curricular learning

Allow obsessions. Kids love a challenge and will immerse themselves completely in something they are trying to crack. Even if you can't understand why your child might want to try to write down all the numbers to a million, get to the top level on a computer game or learn to skip backwards, be tolerant. Seeing a job through to the end is a trait worth acquiring.

Enough is enough! Kids need opportunities and the chance to develop their talents and interests; they don't need to be signed up for so many extra-curricular activities that there's no free time for just messing about.

Play on! If your children seem musical, let them learn to play an instrument and try to dissuade them from giving up instrumental music lessons while at school. It's easy to drop an instrument, but difficult to get back into playing again once peers have become more advanced.

Love the noise. Encourage your child in their early attempts to play an instrument. Avoid wincing and covering your ears! If you are positive, you should be rewarded with rapid improvement and, sooner or later, some tolerable music.

Make practice easy by creating a music corner where the instrument is readily available (preferably out of its case), with a clutter-free area for scores and equipment, a music stand and – if needed – a comfortable seat, adjustable to the correct height.

A short practice daily, at a regular time, is considered by most music teachers to be the best routine.

Let kids play pieces they enjoy rather than ones you think they should master. They'll achieve far better results!

Leave masses of time to get to a concert or show in which your child is performing, and don't make a big deal of the event. Children quickly pick up on parental tension and anxiety, so try to stay calm and reassuring in the face of any pre-performance nerves.

Remember to check that any instruments you hire or borrow are adequately insured.

Choose inspirational teachers. An enthusiastic, encouraging teacher can make all the difference to your child's progress in music or any other subject. When hiring specialist teachers, or when given a choice of teacher, always choose someone who has a happy disposition.

Be beginners together. Why not start a class or course at the same time as your kids so you can learn alongside them? Teenagers in particular can benefit from having their parents on a level playing field, and it can be tremendously bonding to discover a new shared interest.

Build your child's confidence by getting them to take drama classes. Exploring emotions and different situations through role-play can give your child a safe arena in which to rehearse their own interactions.

Get your money's worth. Courses where you have to pay by the term for a certain number of classes can prove very expensive. More often than not, children end up missing classes because of illness, birthday parties, weekend trips away and so on. There is also the danger of your child losing interest after a couple of lessons and not wanting to continue. Classes or sports sessions that you can attend and pay for weekly offer more flexibility and better value for money.

Speak your language. If you have a second language, why not speak it at home with your kids? It needn't be at the expense of the language they speak at school and with their friends – their linguistic skills will be improved if they're bilingual.

Encourage and support your kids in doing whatever interests them, even if those interests differ vastly from your own.

Home study

Go back to school. Learn, alongside your children, all the things you missed first time around. Resist the temptation to say, "It's all so different, I can't understand it." If possible, undertake your own research so that you can widen their understanding of a subject.

Don't do the homework – it's for children, not for parents! Offer help when it's requested, but don't take over. When helping, guide your children to the answers rather than providing them, and try to be patient while they work.

Do your paperwork with your children while they do their homework. This way, you'll be on hand to answer queries and (as long as you don't swear and curse!) you will set an example of quiet concentration.

Plan vacation homework so that it doesn't blight the break. At the beginning of the holiday take a look at everything that needs to be done – not forgetting holiday reading – and loosely schedule it across the time available.

Keep skills sharp. If your kids don't get any holiday homework, make sure that they fit in lots of reading, and that you challenge them to some mental arithmetic, provide wordsearch and puzzle books and encourage them to keep a holiday diary. A little bit of reading, writing and arithmetic in the vacation makes the return to school less daunting and difficult.

Strike a balance between getting your children to do their homework the minute they come home and letting them leave it so late that they can't get to bed at the proper time. Develop a regular slot for homework that suits your child, and at the weekends, take stock on Friday of what needs to be achieved by Monday morning, and encourage your children to make their own plan of how and when they will get it all done.

Stay one step ahead. If your child is struggling with a particular subject at school, there's no reason why you shouldn't work on it a little at home. Trouble with English? Read and discuss good books together. With Maths? Pose interesting mathematical problems in the course of everyday living: "If you add your ages together, are you kids older than me?" "I brought back five Euros from my trip – you four can share them." With History? Learn some weird (and preferably shocking) facts and stories that you can pass on. Enjoy yourselves! There's no reason why "extra work" shouldn't be informal and entertaining.

Play to your strengths when helping with homework, and let other family members play to theirs: Mummy might help with English, History and Geography, Daddy with French and Granny with Maths. Send your child to knowledgeable family members for some intensive coaching at exam time or whenever you think they may need some extra help.

Prop up textbooks with a tabletop bookstand. These are great for children of all ages as they not only display the pages to best advantage, they also screen the child from distractions. Sturdy wooden "Bookchairs", which look like little deckchairs, are popular with parents and kids because they're easy to use and come in lots of funky colours and designs.

Be prepared. Avoid having to reassemble homework equipment each night. Keep pens, sharp pencils, rubbers and rulers on an accessible surface and ask your kids to replace them after use – just as teachers do in a classroom. Children tend to be far more willing to start their homework if the necessary equipment is readily to hand.

Use a clockwork kitchen timer as a homework or task timer. Timers are also helpful for music practice and nightly reading, giving the child a definitive window for the task in hand. Sometimes kids are told to take no more than a certain time on their homework; if yours is consistently spending more or less time than is recommended, mention it to the teacher.

Don't go digital until your child can read an analogue clock face. While your children are learning how to tell the time, encourage them to wear analogue teaching watches.

Set aside some reading time every day. Whether your child reads alone or you are the reader, plan a little quiet time within your daily routine. When reading to your child, position them where they can see the book, then run your finger under the text so that they can follow the words. A three-for-one reading deal can often encourage reluctant readers: for every three pages you read to them, they read one to you.

Chapter 2
Creativity and play

Imagination

Go with it. Children excel at having bizarre ideas: they want to wear a tea cosy to the park, can convince themselves that they are invisible and develop friendships with household objects. If there's no harm in it, relax, enjoy the fun and let them be as eccentric as they like.

Be fanciful. Young children will be delighted to believe that "dancing lady" fuchsia flowers do ballet at night, that the crosses that separate telephone wires are kisses being sent down the lines or that the tooth fairy is building her house out of teeth. These aren't lies: they're the fables children crave.

Invent games. There is never "nothing to play with" or "nothing to do". Teach your children how to invent games: boules played with pebbles, shadow tag (your shadow has to catch your opponent's shadow), sand drawings, relay races (with improvised obstacles and challenges), dances with simple moves. There are more games and activities in a lively imagination than in the best-stocked toyshop.

Make potions. Save some little plastic bottles and help your kids to gather the ingredients for potions: pleasant ones (a mixture of bathroom toiletries), weird ones (strange food combinations) and downright yucky ones (earth, paint, milk, washing-up water ... anything). Stick around while they make them to check that they don't a) wreck your home in the process, b) get their hands on anything dangerous and c) actually drink them! Scary as it sounds for parents, it's a lot of fun for kids to make up potions and invent the magical effects they cause.

Make believe. Take your kids to a palace and all of you pretend that you are royal, go to a museum and strike the poses of the statues, lie with your hands over your chest and imagine yourselves to be ancient Egyptian mummies. Getting into character is a gateway to getting into history, drama and art – and out of yourself.

Improvise scenarios. Kids love simple acting exercises. A couple of children might try having a conversation in which each wants to have the last word, each is trying to impress the other or each is frightened of the other. Suggest subjects and situations that are of particular interest to your children and let them invent their own improvisations.

Share your enthusiasms. Involve your children in whatever you adore, be it making jewellery, visiting battlefields, walking for charity, baking, birdwatching, dancing or DIY. Within reason, kids can get involved in most adult pastimes, and they can really benefit from taking in detailed information at an early age.

Trace connections between your child and a historical figure. A surprising number of children can claim to be related to someone they might learn about in school, so it's well worth delving into your family history. If you can't find any direct connections, seek out more oblique ones: a great-grandfather who once met Churchill or Roosevelt, a distant cousin who was friends with the Sultan of Zanzibar, a great-great-great-grandmother who was sympathetic to the suffragette movement. However tenuous the relationship, it can be enough to make a child feel special, and to give them a penchant for history.

Keep talismanic objects. Allow your children to see and touch the things that are magical to you and your family: a lock of hair from a great-grandmother, an old-fashioned fairy book, a tiny gold charm, a fragment of china discovered in the garden. Tell stories to bring these objects to life in their imagination.

Point things out – skies, stars, trees, flowers, animals, buildings, people, views, colours, textures, effects, sounds, sensations … anything that moves or intrigues you.

Build a cairn in your garden or in a secret place in the park. Gather together a small collection of white pebbles – collect them when you notice them – and on each wonderful or momentous day (a day to mark with a white stone), add one stone to the cairn.

Stomp! Gather together lots of household objects that make a pleasing, percussive noise and "jam" with your children, making rhythms on whatever comes to hand, stamping your feet and dancing to the different beats you create.

Invent your own traditions. Develop some unique rituals with your kids. You might let them eat some chocolate from their stockings before breakfast on Christmas mornings, have an annual midnight feast or pitch a tent in the garden from which to watch the stars on a summer's birthday. Whatever they are, indulge in traditions that are magical for your children and that they will remember for the rest of their lives.

Pass on stories. Every family has its stories, myths and legends. If you enjoyed hearing them as a child, pass them on – duly embellished – to your own offspring. If possible, add a few contemporary tales of your own to the family collection.

Encourage your kids to entertain themselves by giving them books, paper, colouring pens, games, puzzles, construction toys, playing cards, simple musical instruments and dressing-up clothes. Kids have hungry little minds and throughout childhood need a good range of things to play with!

Let kids plan and organize. Children adore being allowed to put their ideas into action, so as far as possible let them devise their own fun. They might design or assemble fancy-dress costumes, come up with an idea for a school fête stall, plan games and activities for a get-together at home or choose and wrap presents. Whatever the task, let them run with it. Don't take over.

Watch wisely. Leaving the TV on throughout the day – like animated wallpaper – deadens conversation, distracts attention and saps invention. If you think you or your children are getting reliant on the box, agree as a family to limit viewing to certain programmes or particular times of the day.

Offer TV substitutes. If you surround your TV-watching children with pens, paper, bricks, Lego, toys and games, they are far more likely to let their attention drift from the TV to play creatively than children in a room where the sole entertainment is the television.

Let them be bored. It can seem more orderly and productive to schedule your children's free time between play dates, classes, activities and outings, but beware of organizing them to the extent that they are then at a loss to know what to do if left to their own devices. Learning to entertain themselves is one of the most useful skills that children can be taught.

Offer your kids your old clothes for dressing up in before you give them to a charity shop or chuck them away. There's no point in buying expensive plastic toys when cast-off threads are just as welcome!

Play on. If your children are absorbed in an imaginative game, try to let it run its course, even if this takes time. Better to let them carry on playing than to take them somewhere to "be entertained".

Ask permission before you desecrate your children's play space. The mess of pillows, blankets, boxes and toys that you hurriedly tidy up might be a space rocket, a princess's palace, a train station or a hospital. It could even be a pit of snakes or a lion's den! You can never know what you are walking into, so be sure to tread carefully.

Words and books

Speak freely. Don't limit your vocabulary for little ears. Even small children can learn what we think of as big or difficult words if they are used in an understandable context. If you think they may be mystified, still use the word but explain it in the same breath: "That dog is really mischievous – playful and naughty ..."

Allow kids' diction. When children are just learning to express themselves, don't constantly correct them. Once in a while it's fine to remind kids that, for example, "Sammy and me went ..." should be "Sammy and I went", or that "There's kids in our class" should be "There are kids in our class", but try to listen to what they are saying before you obsess about how they are saying it.

Promote nonsense. Why disparage children's words? They are often descriptive and apt. Encourage your kids to make up and use words of their own invention. You may find yourself using them too!

Bottoms up! All kids are crude. Older children often find scatology hilarious, and, let's face it, adults are pretty easily entertained by crudeness! Don't worry about it, but don't promote it: try to keep it within bounds and instil in your child a sense of when it is or is not appropriate.

Word games are free, portable and suitable for children of all ages. Toddlers can name objects; pre-schoolers can find simple words beginning with a particular letter; and older children can take turns to name countries or animals beginning with each letter of the alphabet from A–Z. The options are endless, and it's easy to make up your own games to suit your child's abilities and interests.

Play Ghost. The aim of this word game is not to make a word! The first player thinks of a word and says the first letter. Each player in turn adds another letter. They each must have a certain word in mind but cannot say what it is. The object of the game is to avoid being the person who actually makes a word. Other players can challenge if they don't believe that a suggested letter could feasibly follow. The first player to complete a word or lose a challenge loses that round.

Guess the mystery words. In this game, each player writes a word on a sticky note – it can be an object, a name, a place or any noun – and then they stick it on the forehead of the player on their left. In this way each player is "labelled" with an unknown word that they can't see. Each then takes it in turn to ask each of other players a question, to which they can only answer "yes" or "no". The first player to guess correctly the word stuck on their own forehead is the winner.

Find wordsearches to suit your child's age, ability and interests. Spotting words within a maze of seemingly random letters is great fun and marvellous for improving spelling and word recognition. Bumper books of wordsearches can keep children busy for hours.

Appoint spell checkers. Ask younger children to test older ones on their spellings so that the younger ones, in checking against the book, will hopefully learn them too.

Make letters and numbers out of all sorts of things: lines of stones, shoes laid end to end, loose change, dominoes, sweets, pasta, dough – anything. Children often enjoy writing their names in unconventional media and may be more willing to attempt to spell words in pasta alphabet shapes than on paper.

Personalize belongings. Objects marked with your child's name are (obviously) not so easily lost, but over and above this, naming belongings helps a young child's emerging sense of self: "My peg says Charlie on it and has a picture of a rainbow." "Mummy sewed my name on my bag." "My name is here, on my coat!" Self-importance can be a problem in adult life, but it's vital to the developing personality of a young child.

Put up calendars in your children's bedrooms to give them a sense of past, present and future. Start with an infant calendar that allows you to display the day, the date and the weather. When they are older and can read, progress to a month-to-view hanging calendar that offers additional information, such as new moons, famous birthdays and religious holidays.

Create a poetry anthology. Buy a big scrapbook in which your child can copy out or paste in photocopies of their favourite poems. Don't veto their choices. Encourage them to include some of their own work.

Have rhyme time. Challenge your kids to find rhymes, from the easy and obvious ("loo" and "poo" are popular) to the funny (hippopotamus/lot of us) to the downright difficult (orange and banana are notoriously tricky!).

Uphold the bedtime story as a family tradition. After the rush of a busy day, reading a bedtime story allows everyone to wind down, takes the children's minds off any anxieties they may have and soothes them into a state where sleep comes more easily. Best of all, it offers everyone time just to be together.

Pack a book in your children's overnight and sleepover bags and in their holiday suitcases. Even if they don't choose to read it, reading remains an option and they will come to see taking a book on trips as the normal thing to do.

Act up. When you are reading to your children, allow yourself to be expressive. Don't just "do the voices" – do the actions as well! Be wacky and give your kids a laugh; be scary and give them a thrill; be serious and bring tears to their eyes.

Don't finish books your children aren't enjoying. If they have made a reasonable stab at getting into a book that you are reading to them but they are still not keen on it, let them select something else.

Join the library. Get tickets for all the family and use all the facilities. The range on offer at most libraries is so wide as to attract even the most book-phobic child. Keep a box or basket of library loans in the hall of your home so that they are readily available to you and your kids, and are all in one place when you need to return or renew them.

Run your finger underneath the lines of text when reading aloud to your kids. Challenge them to pick you up on any mistakes, then make a few deliberately to check that they are paying attention.

Pretend you've forgotten your glasses or are busy trying to do something so as to get your children to read things out to you: the sports results, the weather forecast, your shopping list, recipe instructions, a note that's come though the door. Everyday literacy is just as valuable as reading schemes in making children fluent, confident readers.

Write back. Most children love a gentle back scratch. Try lightly writing or drawing on their backs to see whether they can work out, through touch, the letter, number, word or image you are making. Take turns to trace messages and symbols on each other's backs. It's a lovely, close way to have fun and encourage literacy.

Have a shelf or a bookcase specifically for your children and within reach of young hands. You don't have to be well off to acquire a fantastic collection of children's books: snap them up at church and school sales or second-hand shops, or ask friends and relatives to pass on the books that their children have grown out of.

Offer a range of books to young children so as to discover what motivates them to read. Where one child likes picture books, another might prefer non-fiction, activity books or books themed around a favourite character. Give your children a selection that allows them to pick and choose.

Allow freedom of choice. Kids have reading schemes and prescribed class readers in school, so at home let them read what interests them, be it the Beano, Enid Blyton or football manuals. The joy of reading is a transferable skill that usually carries over into more "literary" reading at a later stage.

Have two home-reading books: one that your child can read and a more challenging one that you can read to your child. Make sure that both books are unputdownable, and if either is proving boring, find one that's more enjoyable. Reading should be a pleasure, not a chore.

Be seen reading. Children whose parents never pick up a book are far less likely to do so themselves. Set an example: have books around the house and sit and read when you have a spare minute.

Share your books. Show your kids adult books on nature, art, architecture, industry or whatever fascinates you. There is no reason why they shouldn't enjoy your collection of non-fiction.

Sing nursery rhymes. Request a book of nursery rhymes if anyone asks what you'd like for your baby. You'll inevitably discover gaps in your knowledge, and you can also widen your repertoire by learning some rhymes you don't know so well. Having a good number of sweet songs to sing to your baby is a great resource in the long reaches of the night, and a book of nursery rhymes is magical for toddlers. Choose editions that, ultimately, your children might enjoy trying to read themselves (big print, bright pictures, simple layout) and look out for those that have accompanying CDs – great for the car or when you have run out of steam!

Read Aesop's Fables to your children. The stories are so succinct and arresting that your kids stand a reasonable chance of remembering their proverbs: "Slow and steady wins the race." "Deeds, not words." "Honesty is the best policy." "One good turn deserves another." Morality tales can sometimes be far more persuasive than parental advice.

Learn sign language with your kids and use it for secret, fun communications. They'll also be able to make a stab at communicating with any deaf people they know or meet.

Read the signs. Ask your children to read road signs, pub names and the names of other landmarks when you are travelling. Pose challenges, such as "The first one to see the words 'crown', 'horse' or 'bar' gets a point."

Don't let a day pass without reading together. Even if it's only for 10 minutes, have a designated reading time each day.

Arts and crafts

Let children paint. Put them where they will cause the least damage, spread newspaper on the floor, drape them in old shirts and stick around to check that they don't tramp paint about the place – but don't stop them. They can paint on the floor or on a table, but an easel is most convenient. Choose one that also has a chalkboard side.

Channel your child's desire to customize your walls and belongings. Buy some decorators' lining paper and unroll it across an entire room. Provide paints, felt tips, stickers, stencils and whatever else your child wants and leave them to it. The result may be a panorama, a series of cartoons, a banner, graffiti or just a great scribbly mess, but the opportunity to deface such a huge expanse of plain paper is irresistible to most children. It's also a fail-safe activity for play dates.

Discover cartoon art. Get your children a book that demonstrates, step-by-step, how to draw cartoons. If they follow the instructions carefully, they'll be amazed at how easily they can create impressive effects.

Doodle with your kids. Get them to "take a line for a walk" without lifting the crayon or pen off the paper. Show them how you can use one continuous line to write, draw and shade. Ask your children to close their eyes and draw from memory. Creating images with a single line is a simple but exciting art exercise.

Draw around your kids, as they lie on the floor on a large sheet of paper. Then let them add their own features and clothes and colour themselves in.

Draw lots of circles on a sheet of paper and invite your child to turn each one into a different face.

Project your child's profile on to a piece of paper, using side lighting to cast a shadow. Draw around the shadow's edge to get an accurate silhouette that can then be cut out. Use black paper for a dramatic, period effect like a Victorian silhouette. Having demonstrated the technique, let them have a go at creating your silhouette.

Allow pavement art. Buy your children a selection of chunky coloured chalks and let them draw on paving stones. The effect is dramatic but not damaging or long lasting – the first rain will wash the chalk away.

Draw faces on oranges, bananas and eggs – to surprise your children and make them smile. Then let them have a go at creating some comic characters of their own.

Recycle your rubbish. Collect old bottles, jam jars, yoghurt pots, cereal packets, cartons, packaging, ribbons, wrapping paper, greetings cards, remnants of cloth and other arty-crafty scraps in a big plastic crate. These will provide ready-made materials for modelling sessions. Young children adore sitting on a splash mat with all this detritus and some PVA glue, making weird and wonderful constructions. Let them paint or colour in the finished objects.

Invest in a mini sewing machine, if you don't already have a full-sized one. These are brilliant for quick mending jobs and for affixing interminable nametapes. They're also popular with older children, who may want to do your sewing for you!

Visit galleries and exhibitions armed with sketchbooks and pencils so that your kids can choose to copy artworks, or else simply sit and draw if that's their preference. You might also treat a gallery visit like a walk, simply strolling through the rooms, stopping wherever something grabs your children's attention. Offer some ideas, such as seeing if anyone in the paintings looks like someone you know, or seeing if you can spot a cat in any of the pictures; but avoid long, ponderous interpretations as these can put younger children off art for life!

Fun and games

Give your children torches and turn out the lights in your home so that they can play hide-and-seek or their own imaginative games. Buy simple torches which are easy to switch on and off, and make sure that you have a couple of spares for friends.

Deface a newspaper. Give a child a pen and an old newspaper or magazine and they will usually entertain themselves by embellishing the pictures with all sorts of inspired additions. Celebrities, pop stars and politicians will grow horns, sprout tails, acquire glasses and say unsuitable things in speech bubbles.

Have a mad hair day. Buy some colourful sprays and let your kids have technicolour hair one day during the holidays or at the weekend when they've nothing formal to do. They'll love the colours, which wash out very easily, but make sure you spray their hair in a well-ventilated place, and that your child holds a clean dishcloth or towel over their eyes, nose and mouth during the spraying to avoid inhaling the spray.

Sing out loud. You don't need to be Pavarotti to sing to your children – anyone can do it! Kids don't mind if you are flat or can't hit a top C. From when they are babies, sing them songs they'll enjoy: actions songs, songs with funny sounds, nursery rhymes and songs that mean something to you. Young babies respond to vocal intonation rather than to the meanings of words, so put as much colour as possible into your voice and give them a concert to remember!

Make your child laugh! Tell them the silliest jokes you can remember from your own childhood. There are few greater pleasures than hearing your kids chuckle.

Play world games. Ask friends and family from abroad to teach you and your children the games played in their country. Be on the lookout, too, for interesting board games, like Carrom, the Indian equivalent of pool (though played with counters on a board), and Go, an ancient oriental strategy game.

Play memory games. Put diverse objects on a tray, give your child a minute to try to memorize them, then cover them with a cloth and see how many they can recall. More challenging still is the game where the child scrutinizes a room then goes out of it while you make one significant change – move a chair, remove a picture or open a window – to see whether they can spot the change on their return. Memory games are easily invented, so have fun devising your own.

Spoof yourself silly! Spoof is simple to learn and fun to play. Each player is given three counters or coins. Simultaneously, each thrusts out within a closed fist a certain number of these coins: none, one, two or three. The players then take it in turns to guess the total number of coins or counters that will be revealed when all the players open their hands. The nearest guess is the winner.

Hold quizzes. These are very popular and adaptable to all age groups and interests. See if your kids enjoy ABC quizzes, where the children take it in turns to provide a bird, an animal, a country, a car manufacturer, a first name, a soccer team or whatever – that begins with each letter of the alphabet.

Be a card-carrying parent. Learn a few card games and carry a small pack of cards around for instant entertainment. Little ones can play Snap, and older children games such as 21. Playing cards develops mental agility and basic numeracy as well as being great fun.

Teach Patience/Solitaire and Clock Patience/Solitaire to your children so that they can easily entertain themselves anywhere with just a pack of cards.

Prioritize play. Find the time to play with your kids. Dads should be prepared to play girlie games and mums blokey ones. It parents can't be adaptable in this way, it debars them from fully enjoying the company of a child of the opposite sex. Hula-hooping dads and football-playing mums are guaranteed to be a hit.

Allow trading cards. Don't assume that because trading cards are so small – and so pricey – they aren't toys. Older children, particularly boys, often have a strong urge to collect, sort and classify, and cards meet this need. It's an expensive and often emotional pastime (when elusive cards are desperately sought), but if you can help your child to keep on the right side of addiction, a few cards will bring great pleasure and allow them to take their place on the trading floor that is the playground.

Bulk-buy construction kits second-hand or at Internet auction sites, where you can usually purchase a large number of pieces in one go for less than it would cost you to buy a far smaller quantity in separate batches. Having lots of Duplo, Lego, K'NEX, Meccano or Geomag gives your kids the chance to build large, ambitious structures right from the start.

Always read instructions for board games and construction toys. Gruelling as it can be to try to make sense of manuals that are all too often written in gobbledegook, guessing rules and improvising structures can be even more frustrating. If you want to keep your stress levels down, go through the instructions when your children are elsewhere – not while they are breathing expectantly down your neck!

Change the bath toys. Rather than buy expensive bath toys that your child will soon tire of, use a range of ordinary objects for bath fun: a little wooden spoon, a plastic cup, a beaker, a sports bottle, measuring spoons, a funnel, a plastic jug or a squeezy toy. Ring the changes to keep small children happy.

Have bath boats. Kids who are too old to enjoy simply playing with water may still take pleasure in sailing model boats in the bath. You can often buy delightful little wooden boats at the seaside, but check that they are safe for children's use.

Mess about with your kids. Take a holiday from being grown-up and join in the children's activities: run about, play hide-and-seek, have water fights, have a boogie or simply enjoy a completely silly conversation. While it lasts, make the most of the opportunity to be childish.

Bob for apples all year round! Don't wait for Hallowe'en – bobbing is a great game for older children to play at play dates, parties or on rainy afternoons. Try "target bobbing" in preference to traditional stick-your-head-in-a-bucket-of-water bobbing! Under close parental supervision the children take turns to kneel on a kitchen chair and lean over its back to drop a fork out of their mouths into a bowl of water bobbing with apples. The winner is the child who spears the most apples.

Allow indoor ball games. If there's no one living beneath you, keep one area of your home free from knick-knacks and breakables, and allow your kids to play with small, soft balls indoors. Sponge or blow-up footballs are ideal. The children will make a racket, but it's infinitely preferable to having them lounge around lethargically in front of the TV throughout the long winter months.

Don't be too worthy. Allow the odd thing you don't much approve of as well as the things you are comfortable with. So, if the children want to play sweet and sour (waving to people in other cars to see who waves back and who doesn't) or beg to watch two movies in a row, or want a second portion of ice cream, allow them to, if only once in a while.

Techno-kids

Watching TV is OK. If a child has an interesting and active life, TV is likely to be just one part of it. So long as you don't stick your kids in front of the TV simply to avoid doing other things with them, and you know what they are watching, it's unlikely to do them any great harm. Total TV bans can lead to ostracism at school (they don't know what the other kids are talking about) and can fuel a craving to watch the box.

Have a go. Try out your children's computer games and activities so you can begin to understand why they are so enthralled by them.

Search for free games. Some websites offer great free games for children. Listen out for news of these on children's television and in kids' magazines, then take a look yourself before allowing your kids to log on.

Avoid violent games. Whether played on computer or on a console, violent games can affect children's behaviour. Check and observe the age restrictions on any games you buy for your child, and take an interest in what they are playing. You are the best judge of whether a game is good for them or not. Be aware, too, of what they might be playing at friends' homes.

Educational CD-ROMS have their place among books, the Internet and television as an important educational tool. Children who have shown little or no interest in a subject can be awoken to it by a well-designed computer game that combines play with learning. Small children will often excel themselves because of the feedback offered by the screen, and older children and teenagers can find studying more palatable if it involves IT work.

Police your children on the Internet until you are sure that there is little danger of them being exposed to pornographic or other unsuitable material. Investigate software that blocks access to inappropriate websites, and confer with other parents or your child's school about safe Internet usage.

Tackle computer addiction calmly and firmly. If your child's on-screen time has gradually crept up and up, an outright ban is likely to cause a war. Rather, agree with your child a timetable that reduces the hours over time to a level that seems reasonable and fair. This method is far more likely to succeed.

Unplug. Institute some screen-free times when your techno-kids have to down their electronic toys to enjoy some more active or traditional games.

Nature trails

Go on a safari. You don't need to take the kids to Africa! Children are obsessive and love to pursue an enthusiasm. Whether it is birds, bugs, flowers, cars, trucks or trains, take them out on safari to see what you can spot. Don't forget the professional paraphernalia: binoculars, notebook and pencil.

Go dippy. Pond dipping is fun for all ages, but little ones need close supervision to avoid going for a dip themselves. You'll require a fishing net and a plastic container, preferably shallow and flat-bottomed. Put a little pond water in the bottom of the container, drag the net through the shallows at the edge of the pond, then tip its contents out into the container and see what you can find. During the summer months, most ponds will yield many different bugs.

Visit a local pond in the springtime to try to find tadpoles. If you strike lucky, revisit the pond from time to time to watch them develop into froglets, then frogs. Children of all ages enjoy frog-spotting in the wild.

Keep an observation tank. Snails, slugs, worms, tadpoles, frogs, insects and crabs are all fascinating to kids. Buy from a pet shop a medium-sized plastic tank with a narrowly vented top and use it for the observation of creatures that you keep temporarily in captivity. Frogs will need some water with a rocky platform to sit on; insects some twigs and foliage; snails, slugs and worms require a decent amount of moist soil; and crabs some sea water, rocks and – if possible – sand. After capturing these creatures, only keep them for an hour or two. Release them back into the wild as soon as possible as they won't survive long separated from their natural food sources.

Connect. If you and your children are in a wonderful place, stop what you are doing, stand or sit still, and simply focus on sensory impressions. Guide your kids to be aware of the sounds around them, the light, colours, movement and smells. Ask them to describe what they can see, hear, touch or even taste. They may tease you for being intense, but they'll find it rewarding all the same.

Choose a wishing tree. If there's a particular tree your child likes, make it their wishing tree. They can touch it to make a wish. Or, if the tree is in your own garden, they can write wishes and stick them to it, or tie a ribbon around its trunk or branches as a symbol of a wish.

Catch a leaf. It is fantastically difficult to catch a falling leaf, but immensely good fun. Let your children run about beneath the trees on a windy autumn day trying to catch that elusive symbol of good luck. You might even suggest that each leaf brings its catcher a wish.

Make an autumn display of as many differently shaped and coloured leaves as your children can find. Arrange them in a vase or stick them on to paper or card to create a beautiful natural collage.

Play Poohsticks with children of all ages. Once learned, nobody ever forgets or stops enjoying the game. Simultaneously drop sticks into a stream or river on one side of a bridge, then run to the other side to see whose emerges first. It goes without saying that small children must be well supervised.

Skim stones. Collect good, flat, round skimmers when on walks and rambles so that you can then indulge in a long, satisfying skimming session with your kids, competing to see who can achieve the most leaps.

Make snow angels. Kids love to throw themselves into virgin snow. Let them, and show them the magical angel shapes they can make if they lie on their backs fanning their arms and legs. Try never to keep kids inside when snow has settled. Allow them to run about and enjoy it as much as possible.

Grow things, even if it's only cress on wet cotton wool! Children love checking daily for new growth and watching the flowers that they've planted bloom. If you have a garden, a patio or a balcony, give your kids a little patch of their own. If you've no outdoor spaces, find a sunny windowsill and plant some seeds together.

Observe a "bonsai potato". Choose a medium-sized potato, make a little pedestal to support and cradle it (scrunched-up silver foil works well for this), keep it out of direct sunlight, and then watch as – day by day over a few weeks – it grows strange, gnarled shoots.

Choose fun plants. Children tend to like dwarf strawberries as they are sweet and juicy and can even be grown in hanging baskets. Peas also make a good kids' crop as they can be picked, popped open and munched on the spot.

Plant pumpkin seeds in indoor pots in mid-spring. These should shoot up quickly. About a month later, when you've a reasonable growth and the weather is warming up a little, make a big hole in your garden and fill it with manure, covered with a top layer of 3in (8cm) of soil. Take the pumpkin plant out of its pot, place it on the mound and (hopefully!) watch it grow.

Sow your children's names in flowers in your garden or window-box. Plant brightly coloured, short-stemmed, densely flowering plants to create the best effect.

Grow pansies, which look like cute little faces, and ascribe names and personalities to them.

Press flowers. Choose blooms with small, delicate and brightly coloured petals (but don't pick wild flowers) and press them within the pages of a large, heavy book. Leave them undisturbed for a few days until they are as flat and dry as confetti.

Unfold the world. Point out to your kids the natural wonders that surround us: the patterns and colours of an autumn leaf; dewdrops that look like crystals on fresh spring flowers; or the golden evening light bathing a field of wheat. Share your sense of the beauty and wonder of nature with your children.

Out and about

Make simple outings: undertaken with a sense of fun, these can be more rewarding for little ones than grandiose and expensive trips. Take a bag of outdoor toys – a ball, some bats, a Frisbee, a pull-along dog or whatever they enjoy – and simply hang out in the park.

Have a sports morning. Have a regular time and venue in the park so that any children who are interested can play football or another sport together at the weekend. Send a flyer around your child's class to ensure a reasonable turnout. Parents of those who show up can share the supervision and coaching.

Get a training ball for cricket. This looks just like a hard cricket ball but it is made of rubber so is far less likely to cause injury.

Get on your bike. Take your children somewhere grassy and gently sloping to teach them to ride. Don't put the pressure on to get the stabilizers off, just encourage them to enjoy the independence of cycling and sooner or later they'll progress without your needing to say a word. Go out together on your bikes and ride as a family. It's fun, great exercise and a good way to teach them road and cycle safety.

Attend live events, be it the theatre, concerts, puppet shows or street performances. Children are often passive when watching TV but will respond animatedly at a live show, aware that the performers can see and hear them. Kids also focus better on live shows as there aren't the competing entertainments and distractions of home.

Have a city day, out and about in cafés, museums, shops and seeing the sights. Plan a day of fun for your child or, if your kids are older, buy a public transport day pass and just go roving wherever the fancy takes you.

Visit unusual places. Widen your horizons by taking your children to some unusual places that aren't on the standard kids' itinerary: these might include antiques emporia, cemeteries, workshops, follies and other extraordinary buildings. Tell them stories and have some facts at your fingertips to bring these places alive in the imagination.

Break the routine. Families can end up doing roughly the same thing every day of the working week, so it's worth sometimes trying to break the mould. You might have a picnic dinner on a rug in the garden or at the park, take the homework to a café, go for an evening swim or call a friend round on the spur of the moment. Little highlights will invigorate you and your kids.

Take your kids to a shop and buy them something nice. Not every day, maybe not even every week, but it doesn't hurt to treat them once in a while to something they want and will really enjoy.

Holidays and journeys

Get spotting. On long, boring journeys, pass the time with challenges, such as who will be the first to spot a pink car, a caravan, a boat being towed or a number plate beginning with a particular letter or number.

Train up navigators. Give older children a map so that they can try to follow the route of the journey. See if they can be journey "detectives" and spot distinctive landmarks along the way.

Map out the holidays. If your children are out of school for weeks and weeks over the summer, it pays to plan the holidays a little in advance. Fix up some play dates, arrange some day outings with other parents, find out about local kids' facilities, play schemes and summer courses. Planning ahead lets you and your kids choose the most attractive options while there is still availability.

Choose family holidays that allow you and your children to play together. For your kids, having your unhurried attention is golden time, so try to have unscheduled hours together, when you can just muck about. Kids' clubs can be great, but they're no substitute for time with mum and dad.

Find safe havens. Choose vacation venues where your older children can have a certain amount of freedom. Campus-style family centres are great for kids who are pressing to be allowed to do things on their own. Make sure that you know where

they are going and, if possible, get them to go in groups of two or more.

Get the ratio right. Take enough adults on vacation. Two adults to four kids can be tiring; four adults to four kids is far more relaxing. Invite along family and friends to improve the adults-to-kids ratio, and take turns with the kids so that adult couples are able to have a little time together.

Agree some ground rules in advance if you are holidaying with friends and their children. For instance, agree roughly when the children will have to go to bed, how much junk food they'll be allowed to eat and how the babysitting rota could work. It's best to tackle some basics before departure so that disagreements don't spoil the holiday.

Visit hot countries in spring or autumn when the weather is warm enough for outdoor bathing, but not so hot that your children will be uncomfortable or at risk of getting burned.

Make a holiday checklist of things to do and take, well in advance of your family's departure. That way, you'll give yourself enough time to remember all the vital things you've left off it!

Get the pack to pack! If your children pack their own suitcases, they are far more likely to remember to use (and therefore far less likely to lose) what's in them. As soon as they can enjoy going to fetch things, ask your young children to help with the packing. As they get older, make packing lists with them, then let them get on with finding, packing and ticking off what has gone into their cases. Discreetly make sure that essentials have been remembered, but resist the temptation to repack or substitute clothes you prefer.

Less is more. If your child is going on a trip or a holiday during which they'll have sole responsibility for their luggage and possessions, dissuade them from taking anything valuable or irreplaceable. In fact, make sure that they only pack things you and they can afford to lose. Moreover, don't overpack. Most kids will be happy to wear the same clothes again and again!

Arrange for some help with the children the day before you go away on a long vacation. Packing and looking after kids can be a pretty exhausting combo!

Wear new shoes before packing them to take on holiday. Comfortable shoes are an essential for content kids, and the last thing you want is for your child to get sore feet or a blister within the first couple of days. "Wet and dry" sandals, which can be worn in the water or on dry land, are fantastic for the beach as kids never need to take them off.

Travel light. If your children have to lift and carry their own bags, equip them with squashy canvas holdalls on wheels, with extendable rigid handles. These cases are light, roomy (you can often increase their capacity by opening a zip) and easy for a child to trundle. Remember to leave a little space for the souvenirs they'll no doubt want to buy.

Remember to order children's meals or vegetarian meals well in advance of your flight. Requests made at the check-in desk are usually too late.

Tackle takeoff. Buy some sweets – boiled sweets for older children – and suck them on take-off and landing to help to alleviate ear discomfort when the cabin pressure changes. If you don't have any, tell your kids to yawn rather than to hold their noses and blow (which will only make the discomfort worse!). Allow babies to suckle during take-off, or even just to suck your clean finger.

Take distracting toys when flying with babies and toddlers. Toys with lights and movement are particularly effective in averting crying. Other passengers may not enjoy them, but most would agree that they are preferable to screams!

Shape your days. Every minute of the holiday is precious for your children, so give each day some shape or focus. You needn't pack your days with activities, but a whole day at the pool or on the beach can be too long for kids – from the point of view of sun exposure if nothing else. Some families find that having an outing in one half of the day and a rest in the other half works well for adults and children alike.

Make a travel scrapbook of photos, postcards, tickets and other ephemera from any journeys or trips you take with your children. Encourage them to keep a diary or sketchbook while travelling.

Send postcards. Remember to take your children's friends' addresses with you on holiday so that they can send them postcards. This is also a neat way to get them to do a bit of writing over the break!

Make pen pals. Encourage friendships, particularly with children from other countries, and exchange details so as to open up the possibility of the kids becoming pen pals.

Don't be a wet blanket. Children rarely notice the things that annoy adults, so if you think your holiday accommodation or service poor, don't share your complaints with the children. Your disappointments may mar your vacation, but there's no need for them to spoil theirs.

Make opportunities. Make fun things happen on holiday. Out in a glass-bottomed boat? Ask if your kids can take a short turn at the wheel. Watching people playing an unusual game on the beach? See it your kids can have a go. The worst that can happen is that people say "no", the best is that you try something fun, get involved, make new friends and gain some memorable experiences.

Taste the place. Leave your hotel or apartment to experience something of the local life that surrounds you. There's little point in taking your children abroad if their horizons aren't extended beyond tourist accommodation and the beach. Take the bus, visit the local food market, eat in the restaurants that locals frequent, and try to experience whatever is special about your location.

Buy inflatables to turn a 10-minute swim into hours of messing about in the pool. Outdoor pools can be chilly, even in late spring, and your children will be more likely to use them if they can haul themselves on to a lilo from time to time to warm up in the sun.

Take out travel insurance and provision for roadside assistance if you are taking your car abroad. Getting stranded with kids can be nightmarish, so put adequate safety nets in place before you leave. Shop around for a good travel policy, making absolutely sure that you are covered for cancellation of the holiday (not all policies cover this).

Ask taxi drivers and bus drivers to slow down if you are nervous of the speeds at which they are driving. Look up the words in your phrase book in advance of a journey and, if you can be understood, so as not to cause offence make the excuse that your child gets car-sick.

Teach the tides. If you're on a seaside holiday, explain low and high tides to your children and challenge them to work out from the time and tide information whether the tide will be in or out when they arrive at the beach. Clearly point out any areas where a rising tide could cut them off from the rest of the beach.

Getting physical

Why climb the walls when your kids can do it for you? Where possible, fit rungs, trapeze ropes, swing seats and other activity furniture in children's bedrooms so that they can get some exercise during bad weather. If you have the space, a trampette or exercise bike will also prove popular.

Have a knock-up! A wall and a bit of tarmac are all you need for an impromptu game of rebound. Use a bouncy ball and your hands or a tennis ball and racquets, and take turns to hit the ball against the wall, as if playing squash. This is great for improving your kids' hand–eye coordination.

Don't go off to the gym on your own if you haven't the time to be active with your children. Exercising with them benefits everyone. Walking, kicking a ball around, playing aeroplanes with your baby, even pushing a buggy, all hone and tone your body.

Join a gym or sports club that has kids' programmes. If you go as a family, you'll be all the more likely to stick at it and won't miss out on time together.

Prioritize healthy activities over sedentary ones. Suggest ice skating, soft play, swimming, tennis, bowling, Swingball, basketball shots, a football penalty shootout or a trip to the park before you offer a cinema visit, the amusement arcade or a meal out.

Favour swimming over other sports until your child can safely swim a length. Learning to swim isn't just recreation, it's an essential life skill that cannot be acquired too early. If your child is scared of the water, go swimming as often as possible, but don't put on the pressure. If they dip a toe in the water one week and a foot the next, that is fine as long as they make a little progress regularly. Take advice from a swimming instructor at your local pool.

Watch your child swim until you are absolutely sure that they are confident and safe. Don't delegate this responsibility to an instructor or a lifeguard who may be trying to watch many children simultaneously. Stick around at swimming parties – fun swims can be mayhem.

School swimming classes are rarely attended by parents. Be sure that a new school or a new teacher is well briefed about your child's ability, or lack of it.

Have a comfy ride. If your kids try riding for the first time, make sure that they wear shoes or boots with a small heel, a pair of long, soft trousers rather than jeans (which can chafe) and a protective hat that has been properly sized and fitted. Last but not least, request a small, docile pony!

Skate in style. The safest and most comfortable gear for ice skating is: long, stretchy, tight-fitting trousers, a long-sleeved top (jumpers and fleeces are too hot), thick gloves (for warmth and protection) and a soft, close-fitting hat that could help to cushion a fall. Bear in mind that most rinks don't allow baseball caps as their peaks can cause injuries and some don't permit any hats, in case they fly off and cause an obstruction on the ice.

Run children like dogs! Unless your kids are ill, make sure that they get at least an hour of vigorous exercise each day: walking around the park, kicking a ball, swimming or playing sport. Join them and you'll feel the benefit yourself.

Teach playground games that you remember from your own childhood: skipping, hopscotch, French skipping, grandmother's footsteps, oranges and lemons, ring-a-ring o' roses, the hokey-cokey or whatever else you enjoyed. These perennials help children to play cooperatively, and also improve their balance, mobility and coordination.

Clap. Children can clap from when they are very small, and really enjoy it. Play "copyclap", where you clap out a simple rhythm for them to repeat. Gradually make the rhythms more complicated and challenging, then change roles so that you echo their rhythms.

Shake your bootie! Turn on whatever music you and your kids enjoy and have a dance together – the sillier and wilder the better. It's a great way to invigorate the whole family, and allows your children to have a warm-hearted laugh at you!

Play Header Catch. A simple game that children of all ages enjoy, Header Catch is great for rainy days when kids want some physical fun indoors. Two people play: one is the thrower, the other the catcher. When the thrower throws the ball and shouts "catch", the catcher has to head it back to the thrower, not catch it! Conversely, when the thrower shouts "header", the catcher has to catch it in their hands. It doesn't matter whether the return is successful, so long as it is correctly executed with the hands or the head. It may sound simple, but to do the opposite of the thrower's command is quite difficult in practice. When the catcher gets it wrong, the players swap roles.

Ditch the car and walk, cycle, scoot, share a lift or take a bus to school. Work out a rota whereby one adult accompanies the kids each day, or start a "walking bus", taking it in turns to walk the kids to school.

Get to school early so your kids can have a run-around in the playground before school starts. This can be particularly beneficial to young boys who find it difficult to concentrate on schoolwork until they have burned off excess energy.

Chapter 3
Home life

Food, drink – and teeth!

Eat safe. It pays to know the basics of food hygiene (which are mostly common sense). Always wash your hands thoroughly with soap and warm water before preparing food. Wash fresh fruit and vegetables, wrap or cover raw meat and store different foods separately. Keep all food-preparation surfaces and equipment clean, and use a separate chopping board for raw meat. Refrigerate food at between 32°F (0°C) and 41°F (5°C) and freeze it at below 0°F (-18°C). Ideally, defrost food in the fridge rather than at room temperature. Cool foods quickly that are to be stored as chilled. Cook food thoroughly: with meat and poultry there should be no pink meat, and blood and juices should run clear. Once cooked, eat food promptly and do not reheat. Finally, keep animals well away from wherever food is prepared.

Don't be too keen to wean. Health professionals now generally recommend exclusive breastfeeding for the first six months. Since babies develop at different rates, however, you may wish to consult your healthcare professional about the best time for your baby to start solids. Weaning before 17 weeks is always inadvisable as the baby's kidneys and digestive system are still too immature to cope with solid food.

Have simple fare. First foods should be soft, smooth and sloppy in texture. Breast milk or formula can be blended into the food to give it a runny consistency. Start with a very simple food, such as baby rice, and introduce others slowly, one at a time so as to observe whether any produce an allergic or intolerant reaction in your baby. At the age of about seven or eight months, your child can progress from runny purées to firmer ones with a lumpier consistency and texture, and start to try soft finger foods like melon, cheese cubes and fingers of lightly toasted bread.

Serve sloppy meals. From nine to twelve months, babies can eat mini adult meals, well chopped up, and firmer finger foods such as breadsticks and sandwiches – but don't omit from their diet more liquid, mushy foods such as shepherd's pie, macaroni cheese and lasagne, however messy these may be! A toddler who just eats finger foods is more likely to reject moist and mixed foods as a young child.

Let enough be enough. Don't make your baby eat a set amount of solid food each day. Observe when they seem to have had enough, and stop the feeding when they stop eating.

Vary the fare. Offer older babies and toddlers a wide range of foods with different tastes, textures and temperatures. The more varied the food they try at this stage, the less likely they are to grow into faddy children. Try not

First foods

Purées of:

- **Carrot**
- **Swede**
- **Potato**
- **Sweet potato**
- **Pumpkin**
- **Parsnip**
- **Apple**
- **Pear**
- **Banana**
- **Avocado**
- **Pulses (from around six months)**
- **Meat (from around six months)**

to think that because something isn't "kids' food", they won't enjoy it. Try not to serve faddy eaters the same foods over and over again. Put a list on the fridge door of everything they like, persist in making them taste new things and add to the list anything they don't actively dislike. Never give up!

Go easy on soya, especially with boys. Research suggests that boys fed with soya-based formula milk or other soya products are at increased risk of delayed genital formation, and girls, too, from the early onset of menstruation, because of its high oestrogen content.

Don't prejudice your kids by telling them in advance that they will or won't like a certain food or drink. Simply let them try it and wait to see their reaction.

Quit droning on about healthy eating, or you'll put your kids off good food. Rather than talk about it, just present it, and clean out your cupboards to make your home as junk-food-free as possible.

Avoid offering too many choices of meals and don't, at your child's first refusal, offer substitute food. There is much to be said for presenting your child with a meal, expecting them to eat it and not offering any more if they do not: "You have a choice: this or nothing, take it or leave it!"

Tease the tastebuds. Don't give in to fussy eaters – think of ways to tempt them to try new foods without tears or fear.

You might put out a range of differently coloured nibbles and challenge them to "eat a rainbow", or buy a party plate divided into different sections and have a tasting session, letting them blindfold you to see if you can identify the various foods. Sooner or later, they might want to have a go themselves. Fun games (that don't involve bribery) can dissolve a child's anxiety and make trying new tastes less daunting.

Chew it over. Chewing your food before you swallow may seem obvious to you, but it is not necessarily apparent to hungry little children. Most kids have to be taught to chew their food properly. Eat together, make sure mealtimes aren't rushed and set an example of good chewing. If your kids get into good eating habits from early childhood, they are likely to suffer fewer tummy aches and less constipation throughout their lives.

Tackle vegephobia. Give young children an incentive to taste different vegetables by letting them help to cut and weigh the amount that they feel like trying. Keep vegetables visible in the kitchen so they seem familiar, and present them to your children regularly and without fuss until their resistance starts to break down. Accept that there may be some veggies your child simply doesn't like, and award your child a sticker whenever they accept a new vegetable.

Re-present food that has previously been rejected by your kids. Don't make a big deal of serving it again, or force them to eat it, but let it become more familiar on the plate until they taste it – and possibly even enjoy it.

Don't freak out your kids' friends by serving them vegetables they don't like. Rather, put all the vegetables on a dish in the middle of the table and serve them only what they request. Don't try to cure other people's children of vegephobia: you'll only succeed in stopping them from coming to play again!

Introduce new foods throughout childhood. There's no reason why your teenagers should eat only the same foods you served when they were younger. Offer older kids new flavours and cuisines so that, by the time they leave home, they have become culinary explorers. Teach them how to make anything they particularly enjoy.

Go grocery shopping. On-line shopping is fine for bulky, long-life products or standard basics, but not so good for buying cooking ingredients or items that your children might like to try for the first time. Once in a while, take your kids shopping with you and involve them in the process. For example, tell them how to choose a ripe melon, or challenge them to gather the ingredients for a recipe they would like to make. And teach them to check the sell-by dates. Learning to buy good, nutritious food is an important skill that can't be taught on the Internet.

Roughly plan your meals for the week ahead before you go grocery shopping. Even if you're not a great cook, planning a good, varied menu can help your kids to enjoy mealtimes.

Go to market. Wherever you are, and especially when travelling, take your kids to the local market. Talk to the traders, who may let your children touch, taste and smell foods that take their fancy. For fresh, healthy food, always favour good-quality local shops and producers. Imported food is often less fresh and its transportation contributes to global warming.

Buy the best-quality food you can afford. It's better to serve your children a meat-free meal than to offer them economy processed meat, which uses the lowest legal grade of meat from intensively farmed animals.

Be a sceptical shopper. Children's ranges may trumpet one benefit, such as "No artificial colours", but contain egregious amounts of sugar, flavouring or other nasties.

Buy organic selectively. Some foods are more susceptible to contamination than others. Buy organic where it makes the biggest difference. Make organic milk a priority as it comes from cows that don't eat GM feed and it contains up to two-thirds more beneficial omega-3 fatty acids than conventional milk. Organic flour is also worth the extra expense. Pesticide residues are present in a high proportion of non-organic fruit and vegetables, and children are particularly at risk from these substances because their bodies are smaller and still growing.

Teach yourself to cook if you don't already know how. It will save you a world of trouble and expense trying to source nutritious, additive-free ready meals, which can be difficult to come by. Some homemade dishes can be almost as quick as ready-mades, and very easy to cook – for example, omelettes, baked fish, fried chicken and meatballs. You could even try rustling up your own "kids' foods", such as chicken nuggets, using only pure, wholesome ingredients.

Keep cupboard cuisine. Have a good stock of long-lasting cupboard foods that you can raid for a decent meal when fresh stocks run low. A supply of pasta, rice, tomato paste, tuna, sweetcorn, peas and beans will mean that you are never at a loss for a balanced supper – even if you've just arrived back from holiday and the fridge is bare.

Freeze milk. Keep a couple of spare cartons of milk in the freezer. You can then defrost them if you unexpectedly run out.

Get recipe ideas not only from books about cooking for children, but also from cookbooks intended for kids to use: both will usually suggest a good range of easy-to-cook dishes that children are very likely to accept and enjoy.

Let your child make dinner or at least help you to make it – they'll be much more likely to try everything on their plate!

Make pancakes – not every day but on special occasions and certainly on Shrove Tuesday (even if you aren't Christian – it's a great tradition). Kids tend to love them, and they are very easy to make.

Freeze fruit juice. Ice-lolly moulds are cheap and readily available from hardware and kitchen stores. Instead of buying expensive ice lollies, which often contain colours, sugar and additives, make pure fruit lollies in lots of different flavours.

Get pea popping. Kids love shelling peas – a simple task for a grown-up, but a surprisingly challenging and satisfying one for a child. Teach them how to make a pleasing pop and, who knows, they might even eat a few peas!

Offer crudités. If your children are begging for food while lunch or dinner is still cooking, put out a small plate of raw vegetables: carrots, celery, pepper, cucumber, cherry tomatoes and baby corn are all appealing and easy to nibble.

Travel healthily. Before a long journey, chop up fruit and vegetables and put them in plastic containers so that you can offer your kids healthy snacks rather than petrol-station fare.

Have healthy snacks ready for when your children come back, ravenous, from school or sports fixtures – otherwise they'll be likely to graze on junk food.

Make colourful meals on colourful plates. Nutritionists advise combining different coloured raw, additive-free foods for a healthy, balanced diet, so arrange colourful, natural foods on bright, polychrome plates to create meals that look as good as they taste.

Fill your fruit bowl with a wide variety of washed – and preferably organic – fresh fruits. Kids who regularly have fruit visible, available and within their reach are far more likely to develop the habit of snacking on fruit than those who do not.

Offer balanced snacks. On the same principle as presenting balanced meals, why not mix carbohydrates, proteins, fruit and vegetables for a more satisfying and more nutritious snack. You might combine: savoury biscuits with grated cheese, raisins and a glass of milk; or sweet biscuits with some yoghurt and a satsuma. Ring the changes on snacks as you do with meals, so as to keep young taste buds keen.

Have "treat days". If your child eats a healthy, balanced diet and is naturally lean with good teeth, giving them treats often may be fine; but if not, you might want to try having "treat days" – certain days of the week on which they are allowed to eat a little junk food. Limiting treats to one or two days a week relieves kids of the need to petition you 24/7 and reduces overall the amount of junk they eat.

Be stingy with junk. All kids need the odd treat, but there's no need to give lots of treats all at once. If your children want a sweet and a drink, let the drink be something healthy; if they want a fizzy drink and a snack, let the snack be something healthy. If you stick to this routine long enough, kids just accept it as the norm and get out of the habit of begging for double doses of empty calories.

Eat your words. Don't be forever nagging about food. Keep an overall eye on your child's diet, but don't panic if there is the odd occasion when they eat lots of junk food. Inevitably, at parties and on special occasions, children will binge on empty calories, but try not to guilt-trip them about this – they'll survive! The more you nag, the more they'll want to eat unhealthy foods.

Make healthy choices and your children will be more likely to do so too. Your kids will think it pretty strange (not to mention unfair!) if you are drinking cola while they are on mineral water, or you are munching cream cakes while they are offered flapjacks.

Remove temptation. If you don't want your children to eat rubbish, don't buy it. Take a good, hard look at your trolley, How wholesome is your weekly shop?

Use lunch coolers rather than traditional plastic lunchboxes. Like coolbags, lunch coolers are insulated so they will keep your choldren's lunches fresh and appetizing for longer. Look out, too, for insulated backpacks, which are great for school outings because they are easy and comfortable to carry around.

Spend the money you save on junk on the installation of a plumbed-in water filter that will ensure your children drink good-quality water.

Stay still. Offer your children still water in preference to sparkling. Carbonization increases the acidity of the water, and the bubbles can cause bloating and wind.

Make one meal for everyone, not separate meals for the kids – this will discourage faddiness and encourage them to try new foods. At the very least, don't make each child something different!

Avoid suspect additives. Those most often associated with problems such as attention deficit disorder and allergic reactions are: tartrazine (E102); sunset yellow (E110); carmoisine (E122); ponceau (E124) and sodium benzoate (E211). Watch out for sunset yellow in highly coloured glucose drinks.

Favour a low-glycaemic (GI) diet which reduces the daily intake of sugars, and carbohydrates that turn too quickly into sugar after eating. Both of these cause a surge in blood sugar levels, which in turn stimulates hunger. On the other hand, low GI, nutritious foods – for example, granary bread and fruits such as apples and pears, seem to regulate the appetite naturally. A low-GI diet benefits overweight children, but it is also desirable in kids of normal weight as it's good for teeth, and may help to improve concentration and lessen the risk of heart disease, high blood pressure and diabetes. Find out more from your doctor or dietician.

Reject slimming diets. If you think your child is starting to carry too much fat, don't restrict or deny food, but shift the balance of what they are eating away from fats and carbohydrates towards proteins, fruits and vegetables. At the same time make a concerted effort to increase the amount of exercise taken daily. Putting a child on a "diet" is a only likely to make them more determined to eat large amounts of junk food whenever they can get their hands on it.

Calculate the BMI. To calculate your child's body mass index and discover whether they are carrying excess weight, divide their weight in kilograms by the square of their height in metres. If the result suggests your child is overweight or obese, ask your doctor for a referral to a dietician.

Age	Overweight		Obese	
	Boys	**Girls**	**Boys**	**Girls**
5	17.4	17.1	19.3	19.2
6	17.6	17.3	19.8	19.7
7	17.9	17.8	20.6	20.5
8	18.4	18.3	21.6	21.6
9	19.1	19.1	22.8	22.8
10	19.8	19.9	24	24.1
11	20.6	20.7	25.1	25.4
12	21.2	21.7	26	26.7
13	21.9	22.6	26.8	27.8

Don't let your children calorie-count – it's not appropriate for them. But it's useful for you to know whether your child's daily intake is broadly in line with the recommended figures.

Age	Boys	Girls
1–3	1,230	1,165
4–6	1,715	1,545
7–10	1,970	1,740
11–13	2,220	1,845

Provide fatty acids. About 30 per cent of the tissues in the brain and eyes comprise long-chain fatty acids that, research suggests, play an important role in coordination, learning ability, memory, concentration and vision. The body can only derive these acids from a dietary source, such as oily fish, flaxseed and other wholesome foodstuffs, and these are hardly a staple of the infant diet! If you think your child's diet may not be providing sufficient fatty acids, consult your doctor or dietician to discuss whether a supplement might be beneficial. (Look carefully, however, at the source of the supplement to avoid giving your children fish oils harvested from polluted waters.) Our grandmothers clearly knew a thing or two when they ladled cod liver oil into our reluctant mouths!

Eat together whenever you can. If you have got into the habit of eating at different times, it's never too late to start getting the family around a table regularly for a shared meal. Even if this can only be done once a week, turn off the TV and talk. You may be surprised by how much your children tell you over a tasty supper.

Visit restaurants with your kids from when they are very young to introduce them to a range of tastes and cuisines before they get into the habit of eating only from the kids' menu.

Eat breakfast. It's too easy for busy parents to skip this vital meal. For maximum energy and stamina, favour wholemeal breads and wholegrain cereals as these are a good source of slow-releasing sugars. Fruits – fresh or dried – are also energizing and get the bowels working, and live yoghurt promotes a healthy digestion. Avoid fry-ups and sugary cereals.

Take a multivitamin. A normal, healthy diet should provide all the nutrients we need, but sometimes we can do with a little help. New mums, busy parents and faddy children can avoid deficiencies by taking a good multivitamin daily. Consult your doctor or pharmacist about which supplements will best suit you or your children's specific needs.

Don't police parties. Most parties are junk-food fests but, unless you want to appear completely unreasonable, you can't really stop your child from pigging out with the other children. Best to ask them before the party not to gorge themselves, and make sure that for the rest of the party day they eat healthily. Making a stand in front of your child's peers rarely has the desired effect.

Don't bottle it! Avoid giving sweet drinks in a bottle as the constant bathing of the child's teeth in sugary solution can cause a distinctive type of tooth decay called bottle caries. Rather, offer sweet drinks in a cup – preferably only at mealtimes.

Limit juice to a glass or two a day, ideally diluted half-and-half with water. Pure fruit juice has a sugar concentration (of fructose, sucrose and glucose) little different to that of sweetened drinks. The fermentation of this sugar in the bowel can cause wind and diarrhoea, and it may stimulate the production of insulin, which increases production of fat.

Offer chocolate or sweets that don't stay in the mouth for long, rather than boiled sweets or lollies that are sucked or licked for ages and are disastrous for teeth.

Get chewing. Sugar-free gum quickly neutralizes sugar in the mouth, so let older kids have some if they've eaten sweet food but can't easily brush their teeth. Don't give gum to young children (it's not recommended for under 5s), who may choke on it, and watch out that older ones don't do sports, run about, shout or sing while chewing, or they will be at risk of choking too. Too much sugar-free gum can have a laxative effect, so restrict it to when their teeth need it most.

Brush up your brushes. Chuck out toothbrushes that have become splayed and soft, regularly replace the batteries of electric toothbrushes, make sure you buy a flavour of toothpaste that your kids really like and supervise brushing until you are satisfied that your children are getting into all the nooks and crannies of their teeth.

Not too hard. If in doubt about the correct size and firmness of brush for your child, ask your dentist or pharmacist. A big, hard brush may look more effective, but may be totally inappropriate for your child's mouth and teeth.

Supervise brushing up to around age seven, by which time kids have usually grasped how to brush thoroughly. They should brush twice a day – after breakfast and before bed – for about two minutes each time. Most children don't brush for nearly long enough, so you might want to put a timer in the bathroom. Don't give snacks or sweet drinks after teeth have been brushed at night.

Don't pull out wobbly milk teeth until they are hanging by a thread of gum and just need a tiny twist in order to come away. Check extremely wobbly teeth before your child goes to bed to see whether there's a danger of a tooth coming out in the night. If there is, and you can't get it out with a twist, you might want your child to sleep beside you to minimize the risk of their choking if it does come loose.

Fissure-seal your children's adult molars soon after they come though. Most dentists now offer to seal teeth as a matter of course, so it's worth asking your dentist when should be the best time to have it done. Fissure sealant is a thin plastic film painted on the chewing surfaces of molars and premolars to prevent them from decaying. It's an inexpensive and painless procedure that will be extremely beneficial to your children's future dental health.

Household tips

Beware of the baby monitor, which will relay conversation into another room. You may be exhausted and willing your guests to leave, but it's probably best that you don't broadcast this fact to them! Neighbours with a monitor receiver may also pick up your transmissions – and you theirs.

Have a home, not a show home. Children need a certain amount of "stuff " – books, art materials, toys, games, dressing-up clothes, collections and curios – so that they can initiate activities. A minimalist space, however chic, can seem barren and boring to a child.

Have enough soft, snugly places in your home, where your children can relax feeling warm, safe and secure. You might make a bean-bags and blankets corner in your living room, or a cosy tent den in a bedroom, filled with pillows and fleecy throws. Kids tend to get downhearted in houses where absolutely everything is spare and hard-edged.

Warm the bath towels in winter so as to give your children the delicious sensation of all-enveloping warmth as they get out of the bath.

Put up fairy lights in children's bedrooms. These now come in all styles and colours, from classic multi-coloured strings to mini-Chinese lanterns and mock chilli peppers. They make delightful (and not too bright) night-lights and cast a warm, magical glow that children adore. Buy a reputable make, site the lights well out of reach and always turn them off overnight. Put them on a timer if you think you may forget or if you want to use the switching on of the lights in the morning as a signal to your child that it's no longer too early to get up!

Customize your child's bedroom with removable self-adhesive wall stickers. When one craze or phase has petered out, you can then erase all evidence of it and replace it with the next.

Organize the toys into plastic crates and label them. These can easily be stacked or stored on a simple wooden workshop rack that will accommodate lots of boxes. Put heavy crates towards the bottom and affix the rack to the wall to ensure it won't topple if – as is inevitable – kids climb on it.

De-junk kids' rooms, schoolbags, pockets and other crannies fairly regularly, or better still get them to do it themselves. They'll be amazed at what they find!

Keep a good stock of batteries. Rechargeable batteries are preferable for reasons of cost and the environment, but it's also worth having a few fresh ones for toys that don't perform well on rechargeables.

Please the senses. Cast your mind back to sensations remembered from your own childhood: the smell of your favourite meal, the feel of your grandmother's cardigan or the sheen of your bedroom curtains. Try to surround your children

with things that are sensuously pleasing. They might like
a twinkly nightlight, a fleecy blanket, a snuggly beanbag or
a furry cushion. Whenever possible, offer choices and encourage
your kids to develop their senses.

Recycle mineral water. If your children never finish a glass
of mineral water or leave sports bottles half full of it, pour the
expensive leftover water into the kettle or use it to top-up the
fish tank!

Tackle stains quickly. Remove crayon marks by rubbing lightly
with a dry, soap-filled steel wool pad or a damp cloth sprinkled
with baking soda. Ink can be removed with eau de cologne or
alcohol on cotton wool. Gum will come off fabric if you brush
egg white on it and leave it for 15 minutes before washing.
Apply sunblock over permanent marker stains, rub and repeat
as necessary.

Tolerate mess. Bringing up kids is a dynamic and often mucky
business. If you like everything always to be perfectly neat and
tidy, you'll double the work involved in looking after your
children and cramp your family's style. Keep the floor clear
so that your kids don't trip. Wipe up spills and dirt, but only
have a big tidy-up once a day.

Take off outdoor shoes as a matter of course when coming
indoors. Line them up in the hallway or get a shoe rack to place
them on. Children of all ages inevitably roll about on floors, so
it's best to keep them clean of outdoor dirt. Some guests will

offer to take their shoes off, others won't, but few parents take offence if you ask their children to remove their shoes.

Value Velcro for the time and effort it can save you and your child. At around the age of eight, kids should be learning how to tie shoelaces, but they are in fact much better off with Velcro shoe fastenings, which hold their feet more firmly in place because they don't come loose or undone. Trailing laces can be hazardous for active kids.

Get long johns for your boys. Girls can wear tights under trousers, but – understandably – boys are not keen to! Long johns can be very difficult to find, so if you see any for sale, snap them up for your sons. Look out, too, for thick, fleecy trousers, which are really cosy in the depths of winter.

Know your onions! Dress your children in onion-like layers that can be easily removed or replaced. For example, a vest, a long-sleeved T-shirt and a front-opening fleece are a more flexible combination than a vest and a thick jumper.

Buy smart. Don't make false economies by buying bargain-basement clothes and shoes for your children: you'll only need to shell out money all over again when the "bargains' prove to be uncomfortable, cold, impractical or badly made.

Imagine that you are your child when buying them clothes or shoes. Will the material feel soft and comfortable? Will the soles of the shoes bend with the foot? Will the waistband elastic feel loose enough? Will the label scratch? Will the buckle rub? Some styles made in children's sizes are pretty impractical for kids, so be critical and choose only what you can see will keep them comfy and cosy.

Check the waistbands when buying trousers, shorts, skirts and pyjamas. Thin elastic that expands easily is far more comfortable than thick, unyielding elastic that, if it expands at all, feels tight around the child's stomach.

Welcome hand-me-downs. Make known to your friends and family that you welcome hand-me-down clothes and toys. Kids love them as they often end up with a far greater choice of what to wear, and a wider selection of toys to play with. Avoid second-hand shoes, though, as these will have moulded themselves into the shape of the first wearer's feet and therefore won't be a perfect fit for your child.

Recycle your household waste and teach your children to do this too so as to make them more mindful of the waste they create and its impact on the environment. Give them some say in how they discard their old clothes and toys, be it to other children, to a charity shop, a school sale or into a recycling bin.

Choose cardigans over jumpers. Cardigans are quicker and easier for all children to put on. Babies hate having clothes pulled over their heads, and bigger kids can't be bothered to put on jumpers – they're far more likely to pull on a cardigan or a zip-up fleece.

Camouflage mess with patterned, mid-toned clothes. Dirt and spills show up on plain light- or dark-coloured clothes so, for important occasions, dress messy kids in togs that will disguise their antics.

Provide warm and cosy slippers with backs to stop them from falling off when your kids dash around. Children are notoriously bad at putting on and keeping on warm clothes, but if their feet are warm they are less likely to get chilled. Pack slippers for sleepovers to protect feet from Lego and other sharp toys, cold stone flooring or splintery floorboards.

Measure up feet and squeeze the toes of shoes and trainers regularly to check that they still fit. If in doubt, go up a size rather than risk cramping your children's feet. Ask a trained shoeshop assistant to teach you how to check that your children haven't outgrown their shoes so that you don't have to traipse to the shop every time you suspect they may have done. Make sure, too, that you aren't in a rush when buying shoes and that you feel the fit yourself to double-check that they are wide enough, with ample growing space.

Freshen smelly shoes and sneakers by inserting into them cotton cloths filled with a few teaspoonfuls of baking soda, then leaving them overnight. Use rubber bands to secure these soda pouches, which can be reused. Trainers and plimsolls can usually withstand a machine wash on a low temperature (no more than 86°F/30°C). Pack them with newspaper to help to prevent shrinkage as they dry.

Have spare pumps. Trainers can get very muddy and, when washed, take ages to dry. Buy a pair of cheap plimsolls for your child to wear when their trainers are out of commission.

Become a basket case. Sorting out a mountain of laundry can be a time-consuming chore. Avoid it by having separate baskets for white, pale and dark coloured-garments and training your kids to put their soiled clothes in the correct ones.

Dry clothes properly. Hanging out kids' clothes on an airer indoors does not dry them adequately. To be sure that they are bone dry, tumble dry them at "extra dry", hang them in front of a fire or over a radiator, or peg them out for hours on a hot, sunny day, taking them in well before sunset. It is particularly important that babies' vests and sleepsuits are properly dry.

Buy a laundry pen so that you can permanently mark your children's clothes, shoes and bags without the hassle of sewing on nametapes. Keep it where you always know where to find it, otherwise you'll spend as much time searching for it as it will save you in needlework!

Number coats. Don't just name kids' coats and jackets, add your mobile number too so that your child and any carer has your number readily to hand. Young children especially should be labelled with your number in case they become separated from you. Remember to point out to your child where the number can be found, and check from time to time that it hasn't been rubbed or washed off.

Ditch scrapbooks and use A4 clear-pocket display folders instead. Have one for each child and collect in the folders all the precious drawings, cards, love notes and other kids' ephemera that you can't bring yourself to throw away. In future years these folders will serve as delightful souvenirs for your kids.

Save all certificates in an A4 display folder. Pop them in the clear plastic pockets soon after they've been awarded, to avoid putting them away somewhere "safe" and losing them.

Keep square with your kids' cash, however meagre it may seem to you. Have a cash book so that if you take present money from them to bank it – or indeed borrow it yourself when you can't get to the bank – you are always clear about how much they've got and how much you may owe them.

Curb profligacy by making your children pay for non-essentials out of their pocket money or allowances. Open current accounts for older children and pay in their allowance money directly so that they can start to learn to budget and to manage their own finances.

Hold on to the purse strings. If pocket money burns a hole in your children's pockets – or in their teeth – stop it for a while and explain that instead you will, in moderation, buy them any sensible things they request, such as magazines, CDs and so on. Explain exactly why you've stopped their pocket money and give them a clear idea of the terms under which you are prepared to restart it.

The work–life balance

When planning your holiday allocation aim to spend at least two or three days (in addition to family holidays) doing something special with your kids.

Work together. Once in a while, take your kids to work. However boring it may seem to you, your workplace can appear fascinating to your children. Let them do a little task, however small, to give them a role they can be proud of. Explain what happens and what you are doing. If it's not appropriate to have children in your workplace, try to bring home some work that they might find of interest.

Assess your kids. If you feel guilty that you are not spending enough time with your kids, ask yourself honestly whether you think it is doing them any harm. If they are happy with the care you have arranged, there's every likelihood that they are not suffering. Take a clear-eyed look at how they are coping. Are they eating and sleeping, playing and learning? If you've any doubts, think of ways of spending more time together, or free up what time you have to give them more of your attention.

Help your kids first. Colleagues, family and friends often have need of our time, and adults' needs can seem more pressing than children's. But remember (as you are yet again on the phone to a lovesick friend) that – hard-nosed as it may seem – your children must have first call on you.

Plan for the rush hour. Try to have your home in a reasonable state for when you and your family return from work, school or nursery in the evening. Arriving back to chaos can be very disheartening. If necessary, get up a little earlier in the morning so that you can prepare in advance for the evening onslaught.

Minimize stress. Don't do more than is strictly necessary at times when everyone is clamouring for your attention. Sometimes you have to let your standards drop a little so that you can spread yourself more thinly!

Ring-fence some special time. Adult responsibilities erode time and energy, so each day cordon off half an hour – more if you can – just to be available to your kids. Put work and chores to one side, switch the answerphone on, have a cuddle, a chat, read a story, play a game or just let them see that you are there if they want you.

Planning and coping

Make a to-do list if you feel that you can't hold in your head all the things you need to get done. Each morning, go through it, think what you can reasonably achieve before bed, and make a shorter list for the day. (Then be prepared for these "to dos" to turn into "no can dos" if your kids need you!)

Map out regular events on a weekly timetable and put this up on the fridge or pinboard. Each weekend write in the key appointments for the coming week so that you can prepare ahead.

Take note! If there is something you absolutely mustn't forget – such as picking up someone else's child from school – the night before (or whenever you remember) stick a reminder note on the front door where you definitely won't miss it.

Double-enter events in your diary: once on the day on which they'll take place ("Swimming 9am") and once the day before ("Swimming 9am tomorrow"). This is a great safeguard if you ever forget to check your diary first thing in the morning.

Dovetail appointments so that, whenever possible, the whole family can go in a single trip, for haircuts, dental check-ups, sight tests and so on.

Stash some cash at home – not loads, but enough to cover a day with your children. It's a great backup when you find you've run out but haven't the time or the opportunity to get to the bank.

Care for your car. Have regular services and, before long journeys with your kids, check the essentials: tyre condition and pressure, oil, water, and brake and power-steering fluids.

Carry kids' essentials in the car. Pack a small plastic crate with: a First Aid kit, wipes, tissues, an umbrella, plastic bags, some dry food, a bottle of water or some cartons of juice, a ball and whatever else you think might be useful.

Make car travel fun with books, magazines, puzzles and magnetic drawing boards in the back and kids' audio books stored in the glove compartment in the front. Children who are entertained are far less likely to moan, bicker and fight, letting you drive calmly and safely without getting lost!

Avoid car DVD systems as children who are watching a screen lose all sense of where they are going and don't bother to look out of the window. These systems are also a magnet for car crime.

Make notices. Keep a notepad and a pen in the front of the car so that you can make notes to place on the dashboard: "Kid desperate for the toilet so no choice but to stop here!" "Just popping child into the doctor" or "Dropping off child, back in 5 minutes" won't guarantee that you'll escape without a parking ticket, but they will certainly improve your chances.

Carry a few antiseptic wipes and plasters in your purse or wallet. If your kids don't need them, there'll usually be another child who does!

Put back-seat blankets in the car – the fleecier the better – for your kids to snuggle under on cold winters' mornings when you have to scrape the ice off the windows.

Buy big plastic ponchos that cost next to nothing and fold into tiny packets so you don't have to lug coats about during the summer. Armed with these, you can venture out when it's pouring and still have a great time – kids love prancing about in the rain.

Keep a stash of basics anywhere you and the children go to stay regularly so that you don't have to transport huge amounts of baby or child kit each time you go.

Check other kids' birthday plans and the calendar of school events before setting a date and time for your child's party, to prevent potentially disastrous clashes.

File party invitations and events details in a clear-covered ring binder, with the most imminent at the top so it can be easily seen. Rip the top sheet out once the event is over, so exposing the next. This helps to avoid the horror of forgetting a party or losing the directions to get there.

Enter the home and mobile numbers of other parents and friends into the address book of your mobile phone so that you can contact people in case of delays or changes to arrangements. It's a huge relief to be able to get a reassuring message to your child if for any reason you can't turn up as expected.

Check out what's on offer to your kids: playgroups, schools, clubs, camps and courses, libraries, parks and cafés. If you come across something that could be of interest, take a peek, ask for info or chat to people whose kids already use the facilities.

Look out for free events. Most communities offer some fun, free events for young children, and free or subsidized resources for families. Kids are expensive enough without the added costs of entertaining them, so take advantage of free drop-in play-groups, coffee mornings, library sessions and children's classes.

Take leaflets from libraries, community centres, surgeries and health centres, cafés, theatres, arts centres and elsewhere. They are free, informative and often lead to new opportunities for you and your kids. You might also join the mailing lists of any organizations that are of interest to you.

Foster friendships with other parents. It's fantastically beneficial for you and your children to have a strong network and support system.

Snap up ideas from other parents. Listen and learn about good products, recipes, places to go, things to do, strategies for coping and ways to have fun with your kids. But don't bother to compete with other families – just do what you think best for your children.

Search baby and child websites for ideas, advice, consumer info and second-hand sales. Investigate chat rooms so that you can network with other parents and share any concerns you may have. You might also look at some auction sites for bargains.

Economize on double buggies. Most families don't use a double buggy for long, so it's not worth spending a fortune on a new one when a good, second-hand one will be far cheaper.

Buy second-hand uniform. If your child wears school uniform, make sure that you have spares of the essential items as these always seem to be the ones that dry the slowest. Buy cheap second-hand uniform at school sales, or acquire hand-me-downs from older children. Don't pass on outgrown uniform until it is impossible to get on your child, as you never know when you will have to resort to it!

Be prepared. Prepare school and sports bags, and lay out school clothes at night so as to avoid panics and delays in the morning. As your kids get older, expect them to take greater responsibility for remembering and preparing what they will need for the day ahead.

Ensure that your children are warm enough. Even if they haven't wanted pullovers, hats, gloves and scarves when you've asked them, send them off to school or on trips with warm clothes stashed in their bags so that if (when!) they find they need them, they're available.

Trim kids' nails and hair at night. Cut babies and children's nails when they are in their deepest night sleep – usually about an hour after they have gone to bed, though children differ. Use a torch as a task light to be sure you don't cut into the nail bed. Kids who are phobic about haircuts are also best trimmed up as they sleep – a difficult but not impossible task!

Create time zones. If your children are in day care or at school, your time with them will be "zoned" into two periods: the early morning, and the late afternoon and evening. When you're feeling stressed or overwrought, bear in mind that you've only got to try to be a good parent for these short stretches of the day! If you feel overloaded at the weekend, create some time zones of your own: the children might take part in an activity or club, visit grandparents or have a regular play date with a friend.

Take all the help you can get. Parenting is a big job. People like to help, so accept help graciously and guiltlessly when it's offered. To be willing to be helped is a strength, not a weakness, and if a little assistance will benefit your child, there is every reason to accept it.

Show your gratitude to the people who help you and your kids. Care for them, thank them and make it abundantly clear that you appreciate and value them.

Value small achievements. If you feel down and a little defeated by the task of being a parent, try to still your thoughts with practical distractions. Rather than sitting in a heap watching TV, set yourself a couple of small goals that are likely to make you feel positive – for example, sew on a button that's been missing for months, make an overdue duty call or sort out a drawer. Making gentle progress in small ways can be very therapeutic.

Don't be snap happy. Try not to photograph and video your children excessively. Children can become self-conscious if their every move is recorded, and are often deeply embarrassed to see themselves on video. Shoot only the things that matter and that particularly take your fancy.

Build in extra time to get anywhere with kids, and twice the extra time if you have a baby!

Announce target times. Be clear about when you intend to do things. If you tell your children that you'll take them to the zoo in the afternoon, they'll probably want to go straight after lunch and will ask you every five minutes whether it's time to go yet. Take the pressure off yourself by giving a target time to leave so that they can adjust their expectations and occupy themselves happily until then.

Give notice of when you aim to leave the house so that there's a tiny chance your kids might be ready on time.

Forward your watch so that it's five minutes fast. This allows you the luxury of five minutes in hand if you get held up.

Make advance plans for your kids if you know you will have to go away. That way they'll have plenty of things to look forward to while you're gone.

Toys and gifts

Bring a gift, however small, when visiting friends. Children love planning gifts and take great pleasure in presenting them, so allow them to make or choose something they think appropriate. Even if it's not, their generosity will be appreciated.

Don't give other people's children gifts of chocolate or sweets. The parents won't thank you for it, as you can bet other people will also have given confectionery and the child will want to eat it all.

Buy gifts carefully and not in a rush. A well-chosen gift will give hours of fun to your children, but a badly selected one will bring frustration and upset. Take note of the marked age range, favour gifts that they can master unaided and don't just buy things you want to play with yourself.

Avoid cheap toys. For the sake of safety and reliability it is better to buy fewer items, but of better quality. "Big" presents that break within days are a bitter disappointment to kids, and market-cheap bikes, scooters and other outdoor kit can be dangerous. Check for the requisite safety marks.

Shun toxic toys. If you've ever wondered why some "toys" are labelled "Not suitable for children", it is because they are actually ornaments for immature adults! Little tin automata, brightly painted model yachts, mini barometers and suchlike are all risky for kids. In many gift shops such objects sit next to toys, causing confusion for parents and disappointment for children.

Know your plastics. Although phthalates, a plasticizer, is banned in the EU in products for children under three, manufacturers remain free to use it in toys for over threes, despite fears about links with reproductive disorders and childhood asthma. Babies are indiscriminate about what they'll put in their mouths, so offer them new teething rings in place of potentially unsafe hand-me-downs and, whenever possible, baby toys in place of older siblings' toys.

Banish bits. Avoid buying older siblings toys with small parts that could pose a choking hazard for younger siblings. Apply the same principle when buying toys for other people's children.

Give boys Barbie and girls Action Man, if that's what they really want. Imaginative and adventurous kids are often interested in toys intended for the opposite sex. Don't be surprised, though, if your child makes gender stereotypical choices. Ideally, just leave them to choose what they like and will get most pleasure from.

Favour activity toys and sports equipment over computer or craft products when buying for other people's children. Computer games can become obsessive and cause family friction, while craft and other labour-intensive products can be a poisoned chalice for over-stretched parents. Only give plaster modelling kits to the children of parents you don't mind never seeing again!

Choose perennials. The things kids play with through childhood tend not to be the brightly coloured, plastic enormities that parents take out an extra mortgage to buy each Christmas, but objects that transcend phases. Few children will outgrow an electric keyboard, an African drum, a scooter, a swing, Swingball, a trampoline or trampette, a set of good-quality colouring pencils or a handsome teddy bear.

Buy an extra soft toy. Kids can fall so passionately in love with a particular soft toy that it's a good idea – as soon as you notice the attachment – to buy another identical one as an understudy. If, happily, it's not needed, it can later be given away as a gift.

Get a pop-up playhouse. Cheap, easily assembled, adaptable to all sorts of games and usable throughout the year, an indoor playhouse is great fun for small children. Allow them to fill it with blankets, cushions, boxes and other paraphernalia needed for imaginative games – and don't enter unless given express permission. Children love to have little nooks and crannies that are entirely their own.

Bring home an unusual gift for your kids if you go away without them. Find something exotic that they may not have come across before: a miniature magic lantern, a length of sugar cane, a nest of dolls or an extraordinary shell – whatever will delight and intrigue them. As you present it, weave a traveller's tale.

Request a wish list from your kids (or a letter to Santa!) so that on birthdays, Christmas, Hanukkah or other present-giving occasions you can give them things they actually like and will enjoy. Don't be shy about making present suggestions to those who usually buy your children gifts. Unwanted presents waste money and space and can burden the environment.

Have a present box. Out of your children's sight, keep a box of gifts for other kids' birthdays. Then, rather than trailing out to the shops to buy a present before every children's party, you can check your box for suitable gifts. Keep a stash of gift wrap in the house.

Stockpile for Christmas. In the run-up to Christmas, look out for well-priced gifts and toys with universal appeal which you can wrap quickly and present to those who unexpectedly give your children presents.

Store greetings cards and postcards suitable for all ages and occasions so that you have cards readily available for birthdays, thank yous and whatever else you need to say. Ask your kids to choose some that they'd be happy to send to their friends, and add them to your collection.

Say it in writing. Check that your children acknowledge every gift they receive, ideally saying thank you with a drawing or a card that they have made themselves. Little kids can just scribble their thanks.

Take freebies. Kids love to get something for nothing, and some of the freebies on offer can be really useful. Keep a stash of bookmarks so that they are always to hand (kids are often put off reading by losing their place each time they return to a book). Ask for sample swatches of material and wallpaper (great for making collages!), and accept the free gifts offered to kids in planes and restaurants. If your children don't want them, you can always give them to visiting kids.

Encourage generosity. If smaller children come to visit, ask your children to bring out and share toys and games that they have outgrown. And if you don't feel you need to keep them for such occasions, suggest that your children offer up "for keeps" any that definitely won't be missed.

Make words bonds. Be firm with your kids in making them honour their pledges and promises. Make it clear that what has been offered should then be given, and that what has already been given cannot be taken back.

Instil borrower's integrity. Insist that things your kids have borrowed are duly – and promptly – returned. Appeal to their self-interest: if they borrow honourably, they might be allowed to borrow again!

Handle the pressure. Take a look at your kids' friends, their fads and fashions. You may not want to spend a fortune on trainers and baseball caps, but try to be aware of the peer pressure on your kids that drives them to crave these things. Strike a balance when it comes to kids' consumerism, and don't be tempted to exceed your budgetary limits.

Special occasions

Organize a summer picnic. If you'd love to throw a party but can't face the trouble or expense, have a summer picnic. Just put the word out to your friends that you'll all meet up in the park at a given time, asking each to bring a dish or some drink. Take some balls and outdoor toys for the kids to play with. Don't forget to tell everyone to ring you if it's wet on the morning of the picnic to arrange an alternative date.

Have a night out at home. When breastfeeding a young baby, it can be pretty stressful to try to go out for the evening. Instead, plan a glitzy night at home. Tidy one room, dress up, order a takeaway meal and have – as far as is possible – a restaurant experience at home.

Enjoy party nights. Now and again let your kids stay up later than usual to party with family and friends. Let them dress up in something special and make the evening as magical as possible for them.

Take sleeping bags and pillows when your kids accompany you to adult parties. That way they can crash out whenever they want without your having to bother the hosts for beds and blankets, and they can then be carried home insulated from the outdoor cold.

Decorate at night so that, on the morning of a birthday or other special occasion, the children awake to a magical transformation. Even if it's only a few balloons and a homemade banner, the surprise will give them a big thrill and make the day feel immensely special.

See the light. Coloured and fanciful lights can transform a dull room. For special occasions, dress up your home with rope lights, mood cubes, lava lamps and optic-fibre displays. Kids adore the transformative effect of special lighting (which is why you see so many pretty lights left up on trees and in houses long after the festive season). Keep these lights well out of reach of your kids as they can be hot and hazardous. However, where possible choose lights specifically designed to be safe if young children were to hold, chew or play with them.

Carpet the floor with balloons and invite the children to be "balloonatics", running, jumping, batting and biffing each other. Put on some music and you have a cheap and cheerful kids' party activity. Avoid overinflating the balloons or they'll burst very easily and the fun will be over all too soon.

Set a "not before" time. Kids have a habit of getting up before dawn on special occasions, so put clocks beside their beds and tell them that they are not allowed to get up before a certain hour. If they can't yet tell the time, set the alarm and warn them not to rise before it's gone off. The knowledge that they won't be allowed to open presents or start the fun too early can deter them from waking at the crack of dawn. Be kind, though – waiting is very hard when you're little, so let them get up a little in advance of the usual time.

Understand what matters. Parents and children have very different ideas about what constitutes a special occasion. Remember to recognize and respect the things that are really special to them, whether it's a makeover party, a sticker-swap convention, the appearance of a favourite character at a local store or simply a first visit to a new friend's house. Try to afford your kids' special occasions the same importance that you attach to your own.

Think ahead. If your kids have set their heart on some special event, plan it really carefully so as to minimize the possibility of cancellation, delay or disruption. Double-confirm bookings, leave more than ample time to get to your destination, and make sure that arrangements with friends are 100 per cent clear. Moreover, take your mobile so as to be contactable in case of unavoidable changes of plan.

Do them proud. Don't merely attend your children's plays, concerts and performances: mark these occasions by dressing up a little and going out to lunch, tea or dinner with them before or after the event.

Make their day! Birthdays must be special, even if they fall on school days. Tell the school well in advance that your child's birthday is coming up. If children are allowed to offer treats, confer with your child about what they'd like to take in to share with the class (nut-free, of course), and try to drop off and pick up your child in person on that day. Think up some exciting touches to thrill your child: streamers attached to their schoolbag or tied on the car aerial, some party decorations on the back of the car seats, an impromptu treasure hunt in the garden, a mystery guest after school, and so on.

Be party political. Only give out birthday invitations at school if you are inviting your child's entire class. Otherwise post them or hand them to the invitees in person. If the children are old enough to follow instructions, write "Please be discreet about having been invited" where it will be noticed. This will avoid upsetting the feelings of children who have not been invited.

Take it easy. Before you accept a party invitation to an inconvenient venue, check that your children really want to go. If they are just as happy to stay at home or to do something locally, you can spare yourself the time and effort.

Participate in festivals and celebrations from cultures and religions other than your own. Open your children's minds and hearts to different ways of marking special occasions.

Hold imaginative kids' parties, not just ones that cost a fortune. You might: give the kids characters and orchestrate a murder mystery, devise a series of enjoyable challenges for small teams, have a party-piece competition where each child or group prepares a "turn", or rehearse and perform a karaoke or a dance show. If you are throwing a DIY party such as these, only invite well-behaved children whom you can easily control, and avoid putting girl and boy teams in competition with each other – mixed teams tend to be much more harmonious.

Ideas for Children's Parties

Young children:

- Entertainer
- Puppets
- Clown
- Magician
- Animals
- Balloon modelling

Active events:

- Football
- Swimming
- Basketball
- Skating
- Riding
- Tennis
- Climbing
- Go-karting
- Quad biking
- Laser fighting
- Paintball
- Disco

Artistic events:

- Drama workshop
- Juggling class
- Murder mystery
- Cookery
- Arts and crafts
- Ceramic painting
- Makeover
- Face painting
- Fancy dress
- Karaoke
- Cinema/Imax
- Theatre

Special events:

- Limousine
- Party bus
- River or canal boat
- Historic place
- Museum
- Zoo/aquarium
- Restaurant
- Fast-food outlet party room
- Picnic
- Sleepover

Make milestone memories for your kids – a trip to see where they were born, a meeting with a person whom they admire, a surprise party, the chance to do something they've always wanted to do. Such high points become milestones in the memory of childhood. Record the event on camera and, if possible, get your child to write an account, which they can enjoy rereading when they are older. Also, ask your kids for suggestions – they may come up with something exciting and original based on their particular interests.

Chapter 4
Sleep, rest and renewal

Sleep patterns

Turn off the light at night. Some children prefer to sleep with the light on, but scientists fear that this may disrupt the body's natural rhythms and inhibit the production of melatonin, a powerful antioxidant that is thought to help prevent tumours. If children must have a night-light, dim red- or yellow-toned lights are preferable to blue or green because the latter have a more negative effect on melatonin levels. Any bright lights at night – even those put on for a brief trip to the toilet – will be interpreted as day by the brain, causing melatonin levels to fall. Putting the lights out also works as a clear signal to your kids that it is now time to switch off for the night.

Consult Dr Sleep. If you've any concerns whatsoever about your child, the first thing to do is to make sure that they are getting enough sleep. It is the cornerstone of their health and happiness. Without sufficient sleep their behaviour, learning ability and mood will all suffer.

Let them sleep. Whenever you can, let your kids sleep till they wake up, then make a mental note of how long they have slept. It may be markedly longer than the amount of sleep they get when they have to be woken for school. If this is the case, try to bring forward weekday bedtimes so they get something nearer to their optimal amount of sleep.

Keep regular bedtimes. If you have one children's bedtime for weekdays and another for the weekends, this is the equivalent of asking your kids to overcome jet lag each week! The odd late night is unavoidable, but otherwise try to stick to a regular time throughout the week – and even in the holidays.

Simplify bedtime. If your kids try to spin out bedtime – "I'm still hungry," "I want a drink," "Bring me a tissue" or the perennial "I can't sleep" – make it clear that they need to ask for everything they want before a certain time. After that it's too late for requests and complaints: they just have to lie in bed resting until they drop off. Once they have got used to this rule, bedtimes should be less stressful for everyone and your kids should get off to sleep more easily.

Compensate for delays. If bedtime tends to be a protracted event, put your kids to bed half an hour earlier so they still get to sleep at a reasonable hour.

Enjoy sweet awakenings. Wake your children gently and in a kind way. Tell them you love them; tell them it's a beautiful day; tell them they are the sunshine! They're usually too sleepy to be embarrassed, and will be buoyed up for the rest of the day by such a happy start.

Sleepful nights

Play some night music. Getting up in the night is disruptive and often stressful. Try putting on some very quiet, soothing music to calm both you and your baby.

Adjust your clock. Many people sleep more than necessary. It's perfectly possible to function normally on six or seven hours of sleep in every twenty-four hours, so try not to panic if you feel that you aren't getting as much shut-eye as you once did!

Line their tummies. Digestive biscuits washed down with warm milk work like sleeping tablets for children. Milk is high in sleep-inducing melatonin, so it actively helps kids to nod off.

Avoid caffeine and sugary foods. Tea, coffee, caffeinated and sugary drinks, chocolate, sweets and puddings are all best avoided at bedtime, because caffeine and sugar give children a new burst of energy.

Sleep tight. If your baby tends to kick off the covers, use a baby sleeping bag that zips up and fastens over the shoulders to keep them warm and ensure that their feet stay at the foot of the cot. Check the recommended tog (warmth) value.

Take a sleeping bag to sleepovers to ensure that your child has adequate bedding. Sometimes there's not enough to go around and you don't want your child to return exhausted and developing a cold after a wakeful, chilly night!

Bedtime routines

Avoid family fireworks at bedtime, as arguments at night can cause insomnia, bed-wetting and nightmares. A child who goes to bed having just had or witnessed an argument will also usually take longer to settle and go to sleep. Try not to let the sun go down on a disagreement.

Think of something happy. Some children settle down better if you suggest that they think of something happy before going to sleep. This ends the day on a sweet note, reminds them of what they have to celebrate or look forward to and can even prompt pleasant dreams.

"Go to sleep" is an instruction guaranteed to keep children awake. The more they try to sleep, the less likely they are to be able to drop off. Better to quietly reassure them that "rest is as good as sleep" by stroking their heads or backs to soothe them and calm them down.

Explain your absence. After you've given your child a cuddle, offer a reason why you now need them to settle down to sleep on their own: "Mummy needs to eat her dinner," "Daddy has to do some work," "Mummy's got to wash your clothes for the morning." Kids will often settle more willingly if they feel that they are being left for a good reason.

Put the soft toys to bed. Encourage your child to put beloved toys to bed early – and not to stand for any nonsense from them! This simple role play can sometimes remedy tricky bedtime behaviour.

Have a school-night routine so that everything can get done before bed in as relaxed a way as possible. A sequence that works well for many parents is: rest, play or TV; supper; homework; bath; reading; bed. The joy of a routine is that it takes the pain out of deciding when homework should be tackled.

Change the clocks! When young children set their hearts on staying up late but you know that they'll be distraught with tiredness the following day, surreptitiously put the clocks forward so that everyone goes to bed happy.

Contain early risers. Some children have a habit of waking at the crack of dawn. To avoid the whole family becoming sleep-deprived, develop a routine for the early riser. Make it clear that before a certain hour – say 6am – they must stay in bed and try to get back to sleep. After 6am they might read, draw or play with toys quietly in bed. After 7am, or whenever, they are allowed to get up and wake you. If your child can't yet tell the time, set a couple of alarm clocks to indicate the hours, and hope that they don't then sleep in and get startled or upset by the noise of the alarm! Never allow children to watch TV early in the morning, as they tend to wake themselves up to watch it.

Time for yourself

Have a nap. If you feel ratty and as though you just can't cope with your kids, try to snatch a nap – even just a catnap – when you can. Your good humour is far more likely to return after a revitalizing rest. Children and sleep are certainly not bedfellows, so get into the habit of going to bed as early as possible.

Give yourself a break. Leave your children with someone you trust and have a little time to yourself. Even if you're only away from them for an hour or so, you'll enjoy your kids more when you return.

Fit a bolt (a small one will do) to the inside of your bedroom door so that, from time to time, you can ensure a little parental privacy .

Make love whenever you have the opportunity and are not too tired. This may not be often, but the more you and your partner enjoy each other's minds and bodies, the better you'll weather the challenges and share the joys of parenting together.

Nurture your spirit with whatever refreshes you: exercise, music, poetry, flowers. When you feel good in yourself, it is far easier to take pleasure in your children.

Use your head. If you are a full-time parent, try to keep in the swim of adult life by reading, talking, taking courses or embarking on some home study. It's great for your confidence, will make your day more varied and stimulating, and will help to keep your options open if ever you want to start or resume work.

Break the mould. If you are feeling stuck in a rut, try being more adventurous with the choices that are already available to you. Even small changes can be refreshing. Try different foods or drinks, read a new genre of novel or visit a park that you've not been to before.

Be selective. Commit yourself to whatever you feel is really worthwhile, but beware of saying "yes" to every request that's made to you. You can't take other people's kids to school and help in the school library and go on the school outing and undertake fundraising and ferry a bunch of kids home for tea – and then be fresh for your own children. Only undertake what you can achieve comfortably.

Relax with a drink. If you like to chill out with a drink in the evening, save it until after the children have gone to bed. Early evening is a busy time with kids, and alcohol can make it less easy to cope with conflicting demands.

Plan for the morning after the night before. If you know that you're in for a night of heavy partying, arrange for your partner or someone else to look after the children the following morning. You might have a high level of alcohol in your blood when you wake up, so you shouldn't drive your kids anywhere until you're sure you are completely sober. Ideally, drink in moderation so that you don't have to write off the next day.

Relaxation

Spend the weekend – don't squander it! Make sure you don't pack your weekend so full of arrangements that it is as busy as a weekday. If you can't avoid lots of events, try to space them out so that you are not racing against the clock to get from one place to another. Don't panic if your kids haven't got anything planned – entertaining themselves at home is an essential skill that can't be learned early enough.

Turn down the heat. If you see signs of stress in your child – increased bed-wetting or thumb-sucking are classic signs – take the pressure off for a while. As far as possible, avoid nagging and chivvying and just relax with your child for a few weeks. Give them peaceful, early nights and don't wake them before you need to.

Give head massages to your kids. When your child is quiet and still – maybe when watching TV – smooth and caress their hair and gently, very gently, circle the tips of your fingers around their scalp. Kids usually love the feeling, as it's wonderfully relaxing and communicates, wordlessly, your tenderness and approval. You shouldn't try this on babies, you must stop immediately if your child finds it uncomfortable and you should apply only very light pressure.

Be quiet. Kids are noisy, but parents are too. There's no point in constantly shushing your children if you sing in the kitchen, boom down the phone, slam doors and drawers, and stamp about the house. Noise can be the sign of a happy home, but try to be sensitive to times when your kids need a bit of peace.

Teach noise empathy. From when they are very young, give children a sense of when and where it is necessary to be quiet. Lower you own voice and speak to them in a whisper, so that they – hopefully – get the message. Don't shush them when it's fine for them to make noise, otherwise you'll ruin the training!

Zone noise. If possible, organize your living space so that the family doesn't get on top of each other. Doors and floors are great for separating toddlers from teenagers and musicians from kids revising for exams. Avoid the temptation to open-plan your living space – it may look great, but how will it sound?

Play some mellow music very softly when your family is on edge. Choose something that you know everyone likes and, chances are, they'll soon be soothed by it. The right music can be transformative, lightening the mood of the household.

Be a slob once in a while. Break the rules. Lie in bed chatting till noon, make no plans and let the kids relax, then abandon making supper and go and get fish and chips or a burger. Everyone will feel the benefit of stepping off the stress and duty treadmill for a day.

Veg out! When your kids are absolutely exhausted, expect nothing of them and let them relax completely doing whatever they enjoy.

Have a catch-up day. If your child seems tired, stressed and tearful on a school morning for no particular reason, consider keeping them at home for the day, just to catch up with themselves. Modern children can be even busier than their parents, going from school to extra-curricular classes and then coming back to face homework. Sometimes it's just too much and they must be allowed simply to curl up on the sofa.

Keep it cool. Avoid over-sensitizing your children. For example, don't constantly ask whether they need to go to the toilet, even when they are potty training. If you are always the one to prompt them, it can confuse their instincts and make them overanxious. Whenever possible, try not to turn challenges into issues.

Chapter 5
Health and safety

Health and First Aid

Consult a doctor if in doubt whether or not to consult a doctor.

Cherish your doctor. If you like and respect your doctor, make sure that you don't miss appointments or waste time during consultations. Always follow advice and encourage your children to be polite and compliant. A good doctor is a huge asset to a family, particularly in the early years, so show your gratitude through your family's good manners.

Avoid your doctor! If you don't have to take the whole family to the doctor, leave them behind and just take whoever needs to go. Why expose everyone to waiting-room bugs if it's not strictly necessary?

Keep in with your health visitor. Health visitors are not only for the early months, they are there to help you throughout your kids' childhoods. If there's something worrying you or you'd like to chat about a problem, seek their advice. They can offer invaluable support and wisdom.

Get information to help you decide whether or not to immunize your children, and against which diseases. Read, look on the Internet, and ask your doctor, health visitor and other parents about the pros and cons of immunizations. Try not to avoid the issue or delay the jabs because the the experience becomes more uncomfortable and traumatic as your child gets older and more aware of what is happening. Giving them a small piece of chocolate or another favourite treat just after a jab might staunch the tears.

Keep up with the news. Kids' health issues are often covered in the press. Try to keep abreast of current thinking on nutrition, exercise, medicines, supplements and behaviour, but don't believe everything you read. Difficult as it is, parents have to try to distinguish scaremongering and vested-interest arguments from reputable science.

Put up a height chart so that your kids can monitor how tall they are. Even older children love to chart how much they've grown. Choose a chart that they won't grow out of before they've physically outgrown it. A simple chart (without babyish characters) should serve from infancy to young adulthood.

Sleep beside your sick child so that you can feel for yourself whether they are too hot or too cold, re-cover them if they kick off the blankets and be aware of any worsening of their condition. They'll sleep better with your comforting presence beside them, and you won't be disturbed by having to get up throughout the night to check on them.

Check the temperature. The ideal temperature for babies' and young children's bedrooms is 61–68 °F (16–20 °C). Fit a room thermometer and adjust your heating to keep it within this range. Babies should be dressed in no more than a vest and a Babygro and covered by a sheet and two or three blankets, firmly tucked in with their feet at the foot of the cot. Feel the back of you baby's neck. If it's clammy, then they are probably too hot.

Feel hands and feet to check whether your children are too hot or too cold. The body draws heat away from the extremities when cold, and allows excess heat to escape from them when hot. They are therefore a handy barometer for parents,

Cool the patient. When running a temperature – over 98.6°F (37°C) – babies and children need fewer clothes and blankets, not more.

Ensure your child is free from a temperature or vomiting for at least 24 hours before they return to a childminder, nursery or school.

Ban bubbles! Ordinary bubble baths and shampoos can dry the skin and exacerbate childhood eczema. Replace bubble bath with water-soluble, fragrance-free, liquid-paraffin-based emollient. Buy mild shampoos that are recommended for eczema sufferers, use them on the hair only and try to avoid getting them on the rest of the skin.

Avoid perfumes. Young skins can be particularly sensitive, so choose unperfumed toiletries where these are available. Kids who suffer from eczema would do best not to use soap at all as it depletes the natural oils in their skin. Consult your doctor or health visitor about the suitability of alternative types of washing cream.

Moisturize, moisturize, moisturize. This beauty mantra is also the key to the management of childhood eczema. To give your child relief from dry, cracking or itchy skin, slather on a mixture of 50 per cent white soft paraffin and 50 per cent liquid paraffin. It's like sloppy Vaseline, so it glides on to the skin without dragging or rubbing. Most doctors will prescribe it, though you should also be able to buy it over the counter. If your pharmacist doesn't have it ready-made, ask them to make it up for you. Beware of getting it on your paintwork and soft furnishings, though – this cream is very greasy and can stain easily.

Blitz nits. Do periodic checks for nits using a special fine-toothed nit comb to reveal the lice or white eggs. If nits are a recurrent problem at your school or playgroup, suggest that they organize a "nit weekend" when parents can all check and treat their children at the same time so that everyone is clear by Monday morning.

Take a break. There is little more tiring and upsetting than tending a sick child. As a parent you feel at your most vulnerable just when you need to be at your most strong. To avoid cracking up, see if someone can give you some respite from time to time. Even a tiny break – 10 minutes in the sunshine – can help to restore your optimism and ability to cope.

Keep an open mind about antibiotics. Trust your doctor and give them to your children if they are prescribed. If your child hates swallowing the medicine, try administering it with a syringe or mixing it into food or drink – ask the doctor for ideas. Ensure that your child finishes the course.

Try a placebo. Tired children often claim that they are ill and demand treatment from their parents. If you suspect that your child isn't really ill, try a placebo to quell their anxiety (a spoonful of slightly diluted fruit cordial is good), then keep an eagle eye on them to be sure that they aren't really ailing.

Watch for "schoolitis". Linger outside your child's bedroom door to see if the moaning and groaning stop when you are out of the room! If they do, make doubly sure by checking your child's temperature and their tongue – is it furry? – before you decide whether or not to send them to school.

Give medicines in any way your child will take them: from a spoon or a syringe, or – after consultation with your doctor – mixed into food or drink. If you're not getting enough medicine into your child, ask your doctor or your health visitor for advice.

Take note. When giving your child medicine, make a note of the times and dosages given. Jot down, too, the dates of the illness and its development so that you can give this information to the doctor if necessary.

Medicate for meals. If your child has a fever and little appetite, time the giving of the appropriate type and dose of paracetamol to bring the temperature down before you attempt to offer food. A child with a high fever simply won't feel like eating.

Give some bed med. Whenever possible, give a feverish child their paracetamol shortly before bedtime to give them a better chance of getting to sleep and benefiting from a few hours of undisturbed rest. If you give the medicine too early in the evening, you won't be able to give them another dose before bedtime, so you'll face the problem of the medicine wearing off just when you need it to be working through the night.

Fight minor infections naturally. For example, give your kid live yoghurt for digestive problems and ginger for sore throats. Ask your health-food store for advice. If your child doesn't like a particular taste, try another food that treats the same ailment, or disguise the remedy food in a recipe or smoothie blend.

Relieve constipation by giving your child lots of fresh fruit and vegetables. If these don't appeal, the next best thing is a glass of freshly-squeezed juice or a smoothie. Also, give them a beaker or sports bottle full of water to sip throughout the day.

Visit a health-food shop with your children. Buy a selection of healthy seeds, dried fruits and other nibbles that you may be able to tempt them with in place of crisps and sweets. Even if they only like one or two of the things you've bought, it's something to add to the repertoire of healthy foods that they'll accept.

Air those feet! Choose leather shoes and well-ventilated trainers to prevent athlete's foot. When the weather is warm enough, let your kids wear sandals, preferable those with a covered toe area as these are safer for active children who like to kick a ball around or climb on frames in the park.

Serve live yoghurt and probiotic drinks to the whole family. These populate the gut with healthy bacteria, which promotes good digestion in both adults and kids.

Bathe away pain. If your child has a muscular or a stomach ache, try using water for pain relief. Let them soak in a warm bath – don't let it get cold – to relieve tension and ease the distress. Windy babies and children can then benefit from a gentle tummy rub. Use some massage or natural oil – olive is ideal – and gently caress the tummy using wide, circular movements.

Remove splinters by first placing an ice cube on the affected area to reduce the swelling and slightly numb any pain. Then remove with tweezers. For stubborn splinters, sterilize a new needle by boiling it or putting it through a flame, then gently – without your child looking – prise away the surface skin around the splinter to reveal its end.

Trim your nails and keep them short so that they don't scratch or dig into your baby's delicate skin.

Keep a health file for all those random bits of paper to do with kids' hospital visits, test results, developmental checks, little injuries at school and the like. Use dividers if you have more than one child.

Have regular eye tests. Because children are growing, their eyes need to be tested more regularly than adults'. The first checks will take place automatically when the paediatrician assesses the newborn and at clinic visits during babyhood, but from the age of about three and a half, parents need to adhere to a schedule of regular visits to the optician. For children, poor vision that is undetected can present a range of avoidable problems, from falling behind in schoolwork to hesitancy when playing sports.

Leave out your empties. If you notice that you are running low on a medicine cupboard or first-aid essential, leave the container out and visible as an aide-mémoire to prompt you to replenish your stocks. There's little worse than finding that you don't have any paracetamol when your child has a fever in the night or that you have run out of plasters when they have a grazed knee.

Ask open questions, such as "How are you feeling?" rather than "Do you feel terrible?" Questions that allow your children to make a wide range of answers will prove the most useful and revealing when you are trying to discover their true state of health.

Disguise your fear when your child has a minor accident, and try not to shout or gasp. If you can keep quiet, they may well dust themselves down and trot off; if you can't, they're likely to cry, as much out of shock as from pain. It's not always possible to stay cool, but if you can, you'll be able to act more quickly to help them.

"Look after yourself". Give this phrase real meaning for your children. Teach them that, even when an adult is present, it is they who are ultimately responsible for their own safety.

Address your fears.
Check out whatever concerns you, whether it's your child's participation in a sport that you think might be dangerous or their going on a school trip. Ask questions, get as much information as you need, talk to other parents and find out (without causing alarm) how your child feels about the activity or trip. Your concerns may evaporate when you have all the facts.

Announce your germs.
Let people know well in advance if you or your kids are likely to give them a bug – then they have the choice of whether or not to risk getting it.

Medicine cupboard basics

In addition to any medications prescribed specifically for your child, make sure that you include the following:

- **Plasters**
- **Dressings**
- **Bandages**
- **Skin closure strips**
- **Thermometer**
- **Infant paracetamol**
- **Antihistamine**
- **Cough medicine**
- **Decongestant drops**

Before administering any medication, always check the expiry date and the correct dosage for your child's age. Shake liquid medicines, which may have settled or separated.

Bin bad bedding. All children, not just asthma sufferers, benefit from clean, fresh bedding. New duvets and pillows are relatively inexpensive, so from time to time chuck away old, yellowing, stained items and freshen up your child's bed.

Ban smoking in your home, and don't let anyone smoke near your children.

Choose a vacuum cleaner with an advanced filtration system that can consume as many allergens and dust particles as possible, and run it over your kids' rooms more regularly than the rest of your home.

Be allergy and asthma alert. Describe your child's allergies or asthma to any carers, giving explicit information about what may trigger them. If in any doubt about the carer's ability to cope with an allergic reaction, to administer an EpiPen/Anapen (an injection to treat anaphylactic shock) or an inhaler, don't leave your child in their care. Conversely, if you are nervous about looking after someone else's allergic or asthmatic child, voice your concerns.

Print allergy stickers that announce your child's specific allergy and can be affixed to EpiPens/Anapens, medications, inhalers, pencil cases, toys, lunchbox equipment and anything else. Seek out companies that make 100 per cent waterproof, dishwasher- and sterilizer-safe stickers expressly for this purpose.

Shun nuts. Don't give your children any food containing nuts until they are at least three years old. Make sure that you are present the first time they come into contact with any nuts, and that they merely touch the nuts at first. It's also wise to have some oral antihistamine to hand. For kids under five, whole nuts pose a risk of choking, so don't put them out in bowls within reach of children. As a general rule, you should never give nuts to visiting children as their allergy may not yet be apparent.

Quit multi-tasking when your child is ill. As far as possible, shelve or defer non-essential tasks to pay proper attention to your child. When you are busy with other things, it's difficult to assess their condition properly and to attend to their needs. Sick kids need a restful time with a loving parent, so if at all possible, book some time off work and stay at home.

Offer a "hottie". If your child has a cold or a bad stomach, offer them a hot water bottle filled with warm water. Choose a "hottie" with a thick cover that protects against scalding. Young children love covers in the guise of their favourite book and movie characters. Soft toys with microwavable wheat sacks in their stomachs are a novel alternative.

Convalesce with talking books. When a child is sick in bed or has a fever, watching TV or reading can be too tiring, so audio books can be the answer. If possible, visit the local library to pick up a new selection of titles, but if not, don't worry – most kids are happy to listen to their favourite stories again and again.

Tidy up the sickroom. Keep a child's sickroom neat and clean. It will make you and your child feel a little better if things are orderly and fresh. Ensure that the room is well ventilated but warm. Brighten it with a plant or some pretty flowers (although avoid heavily pollinated ones) and put beloved soft toys well within reach in case your child needs them for comfort.

Look after your own health: your children rely on you! Consider the state health provision in your area and the reality of whether it would work for you and your family. If you think it would, no problem; if you don't, you might want to rethink your financial priorities.

Go hill training. Ditch the car and get fit by pushing the buggy uphill. It's fantastic exercise for the bottom muscles.

Squeeze! Many mums know that it's advisable to do pelvic floor exercises soon after having a baby. But carrying around heavy babies and toddlers can also take its toll on pelvic muscles, so mums should continue to do the exercises long after the immediate post-natal period: fifty a day is a good target.

Mind your back. To give your back a rest, invest in a baby-sling or specially designed rucksack to carry your child around in.

Walk tall. When lifting, pushing or playing with your children, be mindful of your posture. Relax your shoulders, keep your back straight and tilt your pelvis back slightly so that your tum and bottom are tucked in. Make sure that you always bend your knees when lifting your kids – so you'll be able to continue to lift them!

Emergencies

Help before you blame. Focus on the injured child – don't leave them bleeding and in shock while you shout at whoever caused the injury!

Prevent avoidable accidents with some hard-and-fast ground rules such as: don't touch pets, particularly dogs you don't know; don't run up or down stairs; don't go outside without an adult's permission. Look ahead, anticipate hazards and alert your kids to them so that disasters can be averted.

Take a few basic things if you have to rush your child to the accident and emergency department of a hospital. If you have time, you might grab a bottle of water, a blanket, a small cushion and something to entertain your child – if they are up to being distracted. But if you don't have time, just go.

Escape fire. Consider how you and your children would escape a fire in your home. If you have no fire escape or other means of safe exit, call your local fire station for advice. A fire-escape ladder can be a sensible option for homes with an upper storey, and harnesses can be purchased to allow you to strap babies and younger children to your body while descending. Always store door keys and window locks where they can be easily accessed in an emergency.

Know Dr ABC

This handy acronym will help you to remember the correct sequence of checks in case of a medical emergency:

- **D   DANGER (is it safe to go near or touch the child?)**
- **r   RESPONSE (can the child hear you?)**

- **A   AIRWAY (is it clear or obstructed?)**
- **B   BREATHING (look listen and feel)**
- **C   CIRCULATION (check pulse)**

Ideally, sign up for a First Aid course so as to learn the proper reactions to these indications.

Keep calm. In an emergency try not to panic your child. It will only make it far more difficult for you to take appropriate action.

Immerse burns and scalds under cold running water for at least ten minutes. This can be very uncomfortable and your child is likely to cry, but try not to give up sooner. (Tight clothing should be removed first.) Use clean, non-fluffy gauze or a cloth to cover the burn and prevent infection. Serious burns require urgent and immediate medical attention.

Safety at home

Fit smoke alarms and carbon monoxide detectors, being sure to install them correctly in all the appropriate places. Test smoke alarms regularly to check that they are functioning properly. Consider packing a smoke alarm in your luggage when you are staying away from home. This may seem over the top, but if your hosts don't have one, you and your children are in as much danger as if you didn't have alarms in your home.

Choose your furniture carefully. Low, soft-all-over sofas in dark colours (so that stains don't show!) are in; cream canvas upright chairs are out. Robust wooden bookshelves with enclosed shelf ends are in; protruding glass shelves are out. Before buying new furniture, consider it from a child-safety perspective.

Tackle the topple. Chests of drawers can easily topple when too many drawers are pulled out at the same time. Small children have been crushed and killed by heavy furniture so, for a start, always put heavy objects in the lowest drawers. Ideally, get hold of some non-tip furniture straps, which tether the back of the furniture to the wall. Until you can do this, lock the doors of rooms where there is a toppling hazard.

Fit stair gates that are designed without the fixed bottom bars that adults and children so often trip over.

Give away glass tables. As soon your child can cruise around holding on to the furniture, it's time to get rid of your glass tables. If your child doesn't damage themselves on the edges, sooner or later they'll have a go at jumping on them!

Have enough side tables so that hot cups and fragile glasses aren't put down on the floor, and site these tables out of reach of little ones.

Mask sharp corners with corner guards or improvised solutions, such as Blu Tack covered with masking tape (not attractive, but effective), or – if edges need to be covered temporarily – a pillow or a cushion.

Use socket covers. A cheap safety essential for every home with young children, they look like thin plastic plugs and cover sockets completely, making them impenetrable to prying fingers.

Keep flexes well out of reach, particularly the flex for the kettle, and site the kettle itself as far back as possible from the edge of the kitchen surface.

Position catches on front and back doors well out of the reach of small children, especially if you live near a road. Make sure that everybody visiting the house knows not to leave these doors ajar. As soon as your children are old enough to understand, teach them not to open front or back doors, either in their own home or in other people's.

Site door bolts or locks where small children can't reach them. This is especially important in lavatories and bathrooms.

Set radiators so that they can't get scalding hot. If this isn't possible, box them in with well-ventilated covers.

Use a hob guard – a low rail that runs around the edge of the hob – to prevent saucepans from being knocked or pulled off by children.

Turn off hob rings and ovens before you lift the food. Doing this as a matter of routine lessens the danger of leaving these appliances on.

Turn saucepan handles towards the back of the cooker so that there's no danger of children grabbing at them and tipping the contents of the pans over themselves.

Cover cooker knobs if they are within reach of an inquisitive toddler. Plastic covers can be bought that clip over each knob to deter little fingers, but can easily be removed by adult hands.

Low ovens are a hazard for all children as the doors can get dangerously hot. If planning a new kitchen, site the oven high up, out of reach. If stuck with a low oven, it is possible to buy a guard, but these can be difficult to obtain and affix. The best policy is not to allow small children into the kitchen while you are cooking or while the oven is still hot.

Fit fixed fireguards that children can't move. Ensure that these are positioned sufficiently far from the fire so as not to become dangerously hot.

Use safety equipment consistently, rather than just when you think the kids are around. For example, a fireguard is most useful when you aren't there to check it's in place!

Cover glass surfaces, such as glass door panels, with self-adhesive safety glass film to prevent the glass from shattering in an accident.

Have a roll of safety mesh that you can use at home or anywhere else you see an avoidable danger for your young child: widely spaced banisters, sudden changes in floor level, gardens without gates or unsafe rooms that lack doors to keep children out.

Keep one step ahead of your child's mobility and curiosity. Fit child-locks to cupboards and drawers containing cleaning fluids, sharp knives and DIY materials, and keep these locks on until your child is able to read and take notice of safety warnings.

Renovate with care. If you have major works taking place in your home, be mindful of the health and safety implications for your kids: dust, fumes, power tools and other equipment are all hazardous. Be aware of the extreme danger posed by the dismantling of old asbestos or the stripping of lead-based paints. Ideally, get a professional assessment of the health risks before undertaking any work, especially if you are renovating an older property, which is more likely to contain toxic materials.

Paint safely. It's best not to have children around when you decorate using solvent-based (oil) paints. Arrange to decorate when your kids are staying away, or keep internal doors shut and windows open to protect them from the fumes. You might also consider using alternative, water-based paints.

Pour cold water before hot when running a bath, so that it never gets boiling hot. Keep the bathroom door closed until you've got it to the right temperature. It's not just toddlers who need to be watched in the bath – older children, up to the age of seven or eight can wreak havoc by turning on taps and causing flooding.

Lower the lid. With young children in the house it's important to remember to put down the loo seat!

Buy new mattresses for Moses baskets and cots, ideally with ventilation holes at the head. Babies shouldn't use pillows, and cot bumpers (padded cot surrounds) should be properly secured, with no trailing ends.

Read the leaflets that accompany safety equipment, and make sure you fully understand them. The best equipment, if misused, can be worse than useless.

Fit universal window locks that allow windows to be opened wide enough for ventilation but not so wide that a child could fall through. Even if you are intending to be in the room with your young children, don't open windows within their reach – you could get distracted or called out of the room and forget to close them.

Loop up blind and curtain cords so they are out of the reach of children. Toddlers are particularly at risk of getting twisted up in these, so even cords with "safe" ends (that easily come apart) need to be tucked well away where they can't be played with.

Secure your baby properly – every time! Always use the straps of the high chair or bouncing chair.

Store plastic bags out of your children's reach and never allow them to be used as props for games.

Put pets second. If you have any doubts about whether your pet poses a threat to your baby, or whether your child is allergic to it, get rid of the animal. Kids must come first. Always site pet food and litter trays where small children can't reach them.

Be safe outside. If you leave your baby alone in the garden, cover the pram with an insect net and shoo away any cats that approach.

Lock sheds and garden doors.

Don't spray your garden with pesticide, weed killer or fertilizer on a day when your kids will be playing in it. Also, avoid putting down slug pellets if there's a danger that toddlers might eat them!

Fence around or cover over water features such as ponds, which can be extremely hazardous to young children. Sandpits, too, should be covered when not in use.

Buy non-toxic plants. Always check that the plants you buy aren't harmful to inquisitive children.

Other people

Never be polite at the expense of your child's safety. If you have concerns about anything to do with their welfare, speak out, check out and sort out whatever is worrying you.

Be clear with anyone caring for your child. Gently let them know what is and what isn't acceptable to you.

Trust your instincts about babysitters, childminders, nannies and anyone else caring for your children. If you have any doubts, check them out. Ask other parents how they seem when you are not around and, if your child is old enough, find out from the horse's mouth what goes on in your absence.

Leave your details with anyone caring for your child: an address and phone number where you can be contacted, your mobile number/s, your doctor's number and any special instructions for while you are away.

Follow their instincts. If your children are wary of particular people, try to work out why. They may have good reason not to warm to certain individuals, so don't try to force conviviality where none exists.

Complain! If you come across something that's clearly dangerous for children, say so. Whether it's road markings, school apparatus, toys or baby equipment, make a fuss until it's sorted out. Other parents will thank you for it.

Discuss "stranger danger". As soon as you think your kids are old enough to understand, explain to them honestly the danger that older children and adults can pose. Tell them, as clearly as possible, what adults shouldn't do. Explain that if anyone says "don't tell", tell is exactly what they must do.

Suss out sleepovers. Get to know a family pretty well before you let your children sleep over at their home. Be mindful that dads and granddads aren't the only people you need to feel comfortable with – big brothers (who may not yet fully understand their own instincts and impulses) can pose a greater danger.

Go two by two. It is safer for kids to go in twos (or with an adult) to public toilets.

Don't pick arguments, even justified arguments, when in charge of your children. If a stranger is rude to you, don't take them on, just let it pass, or you risk embroiling your kids in a fight.

Roads and cars

Control road rage. Do what you tell your kids to do: count to 10 to avoid blowing your top!

Never walk a child straight across a road, even if you can see that it is clear of traffic. If you always stop at the kerb, look left and right and then walk calmly and purposefully straight across, this routine should become second nature to your child. With younger children, articulate what you are doing to make them aware that it is a road and a potential danger.

Shout "freeze". Rehearse with your children the simple scenario of their being about to step into danger – on to a road, over a drop, or whatever. When you shout "freeze" they have to stand still and not move a muscle. You may think that "stop" would be more direct, but it's a word they hear so often ("stop picking your nose", "stop eating with your mouth open") that they may not pay as much attention to it as to a word specifically designated to mean danger. Your children may enjoy rehearsing "freeze", but don't use it as a game thereafter. Save it for emergencies, making sure from time to time that they have remembered the "freeze" code.

Put children first. Children don't walk as purposefully as adults: they dawdle and dream, and tend to lag behind their parents. Difficult as it can be to keep your kids beside or in front of you, it is clearly far safer to have them in your sight at all times. Moreover, other people's children are less predictable than your own, so for their safety and your sanity, always keep them where you can see them easily.

Respect the green man, however tedious it is to have to wait. If you don't, your children won't either. And we may think that the meaning of these signs is self-evident, but it isn't: they need to be explained to kids.

Walk kids on the inside of the pavement. Teach them to keep well away from the kerbside at all times.

Check your child's car seat is of the correct size and that its recommended weight limit is not exceeded. Car seats should be bought new so as to ensure that their safety has not been compromised by a previous owner. They are not an item to scrimp on. Always buy a reputable make after carefully reading the safety claims of the different models, and ensure you clearly understand the directions for use right from the outset. Never use a car seat in a front passenger seat that is equipped with an airbag. Children should sit in the back of the car in a booster seat until they are at least 4ft 9ins (1.45m) tall.

Master seat belts, which are notoriously difficult to use correctly. They plug into the wrong socket, lock, twist and slip. It's worth double-checking that a child in a booster or with no car seat has put theirs on correctly, in the right position, with the lap strap at the base of the stomach and the shoulder strap tethered just above the shoulder. If this cannot be achieved, a belt guide is a cheap essential. During a journey, check from time to time that your child is still properly positioned and well secured.

Keep child locks on rear car doors even after your own children can be relied upon not to open them absent-mindedly. Their friends may not be so reliable!

Recirculate the air in the car when sitting in traffic jams or travelling behind a vehicle that's spewing out fumes. In particular, children with asthma should not sit in a confined, polluted space. Similarly, keep kids away from active exhausts: if you are at a bus stop or talking on the pavement, move buggies and older kids so that they aren't directly behind belching cars.

Use blow-up neck pillows. These are fun and comfortable and will prop up lolling heads when your kids fall asleep in the car.

Don't argue with your children while driving. Even if you have missed the turning and are lost and late, wait until you have stopped the car before letting off steam. If it helps, take the pressure off by phoning ahead to warn that you will be late.

Drive safely. This beats any safety features. A crying baby, fractious child or carload of screaming kids can be stupendously distracting. Whenever possible, pull over before you try to deal with the fracas.

Outings and travel

Always secure the straps on the buggy or stroller, however short the stroll – otherwise, if you hit a stone or the curb, your child will hit the ground.

Keep your mobile on and within earshot. You and your children will both be more relaxed if you are always contactable, and older children can be allowed a little more freedom if you are just a phone call away. Ask your kids to send you updates and confirmations by text.

Give mobile phones only to children who need them for safety reasons, and limit their use to essential calls only. Seek out models with a loudspeaker function, which allows them to be held at arm's length. Enter your number and those of other key people as speed dials in your children's phones.

Teach your kids their address and telephone number as soon as they are old enough to retain this info. From time to time ask them to repeat the details to you so that you can check they have remembered them correctly.

Write on your kids! If you are in a busy place where there's a danger that you could become separated from your children, write your mobile number on their hands and tell them what you are doing. When looking after a group of children, sticker them with your mobile number (but for safety reasons don't write their names on the stickers).

Do a headcount at regular intervals when travelling with a group of kids. It goes without saying that you should do the first headcount before you set off!

Have a "lost" routine. As soon as your children are old enough to understand, give them simple instructions about what to do should they become separated from you. Repeat the drill to them until you are sure they clearly understand it: "Don't worry, stay where you are, don't wander off, don't cross a road, look out for a person in authority (such as a policeman), a woman or a couple and ask them for help. Remember that my mobile phone number is written on your hand."

Make clear arrangements. If you separate from another adult when you are out, make sure you clearly articulate who has the children, otherwise there's a danger of each adult thinking that they have gone with the other. It has happened!

Lift off together. It's fun to have a stairs-versus-lift race, but make sure that any kids in the lift have an adult with them in case of breakdowns or unsavoury strangers.

Don't let children disappear in someone else's house without first checking for safety. This may seem cheeky, but your hosts may not have closed upstairs windows or covered open fires.

Take a baby monitor with you whenever you and your children are likely to stay the night somewhere. That way, you can check that they are fine without getting up in the night.

Stick together. When walking with small children, encourage them to hold hands. This has the benefit of keeping them walking in the same direction!

Get on your bike with your kids. Find some safe cycle paths (rather than roads), get yourselves togged up with helmets and reflector strips, and enjoy companionable rides together. If available in your area, a cycling proficiency course can be a fun way to improve skills and learn about safety.

Be safety-conscious. For biking, scooting, roller blading or skating, and skateboarding, a helmet is key safety kit. Some children will accept knee and elbow pads, others will resist them, but if you feel that they are necessary, insist upon them as a condition of play. Use mouth guards for boxing, karate, rugby – or any sport that you think poses the risk of mouth injury. Don't economize on protective gear for your children – that would be the ultimate false economy.

Take along enough medication on trips so as not to run out of essentials if, for any reason, you are delayed.

Get beach savvy. For a really enjoyable day on the beach, go equipped with decent sun protection. Take the usual defences – sunscreen, sunglasses and hats (legionnaire's style, with a neck flap, are best) – but you might also try sun-protection suits for the kids, which can filter out around 80 percent of harmful UVA rays. Swim shoes are also useful as they help to protect feet from the sun and remove kids' fear of stepping on unknown objects in the water. UV protective beach tents make great dens, and are an ideal place to keep babies out of the rays.

Put function before fashion. Sleeveless T-shirts and dresses can look cute as summerwear, but they are not at all suitable for days in the sun. Clothes with short sleeves are infinitely preferable as they help to protect children's shoulders from getting sunburnt (only about 30 percent of the sun's rays can penetrate loosely woven fabrics like T-shirt cotton).

Recognize the sun's strength. Babies under six months should be kept out of direct sunlight. Fair-skinned children who never tan but only burn should use a sunscreen of sun protection factor (SPF) 30 or above for even the briefest exposure, and all other children should put on a sunscreen with an SPF of at least 15. Children can safely share adult sunscreens and can also use sun-protective lip coating that contains PABA (para-aminobenzoic acid). For recommended exposure times, consult the packaging of the specific sunscreen you are using. Note that cloud cover only offers about a 30 per cent reduction in the strength of the sun's rays, that water, sand and snow can reflect rays upwards (under sunshades) and that the strength of the sun increases by 4 per cent per 1,000 feet above sea level.

Suss out the sun. If you are going on a journey, work out which side of the car will get the most direct sunlight and, if possible, put your baby or child on the other side. For added protection, and if you have more than one child, use sun visors that stick to the windows with suckers to filter the rays.

Position your paddling pool half in the sun and half in the shade, or else use a large umbrella to provide some shade over one part of it.

Brief your children's carers to be as sun savvy as you are. Don't assume that they'll automatically know how to protect your children. It's wise to take them through the full sun drill, from the necessity for hats and sunglasses to sunscreen factors and exposure times.

Use once-a-day sun filter if you are not going to be with your child and don't have faith that others will reapply sunblock throughout the day. Choose the highest factor available and apply it all over your child before they dress in the morning – don't forget to cover their ears, nose and forehead. P20, a popular brand, should be applied 90 minutes before sun exposure, after which it claims to retain about 90 per cent of its effectiveness against UVB rays throughout the day, even when your child is swimming; however, its protection against UVA rays is only "moderate".

Don't let your kids get sunburned. But, if, despite your best efforts they do get sore, relieve sunburn with camomile lotion or after-sun soothing gel. Ask your pharmacist for the best available. Plain yoghurt can also be effective.

Choose stylish or fun sunglasses so that your kids will wear them. Sunglasses should be of good quality, offering at least 99, preferably 100 per cent protection from UVA and UVB rays. **167**

Kids' habits

Let go. Many children go though phases of hyper-anxiety about going to the toilet. Some go with alarming frequency and others will wait and hold on until they wet themselves. While children are learning to negotiate the tricky psychological terrain of when and how to "let go", avoid making a big deal of anything to do with the toilet. Guilt, shame or anxiety can make unsettled behaviours all the more pronounced.

Get your kids to go to the loo before a long journey, but not before every tiny outing. Accidents will happen, but they are more likely if kids are nervous about the possibility of wetting themselves. Small children need to learn control, which they can't do if you are constantly telling them when they need to try to go.

Lift the lid on poor toilet habits. Put a funny notice up in the loo: "Bradley, if you pee all over the seat again, we'll make you sit in a bowl of gunge!" "Katie, if you don't wipe your bottom properly, we will send you to the dry-cleaners." Only write what you think your children can handle with good humour, and don't embarrass them by sharing the joke with strangers.

Don't complain about bedwetting or make children feel guilty about it. Instead, subtly restrict drinks at bedtime, make sure your child has been to the loo last thing before going off to sleep and put them on again if they wake up in the night. Don't fuss, as it will only make the problem worse.

Use a wet-and-dry sheet. Minimize the disruption of bedwetting by buying a protective sheet (plus a spare) that you can put on top of the cot or bed sheet. Made of absorbent cotton backed with polyurethane, this sheet can be whipped off the bed and replaced with the spare one, so that your child can quickly get back in and off to sleep again.

Black-back your curtains. Young children hate going to bed when it's light outside, but love getting up at dawn. Give everyone the chance of some decent sleep by buying blackout curtains for your children's rooms.

See eye to eye. If your child has a fringe, trim it regularly to stop it flopping over their eyes. A child who is constantly flicking back hair or looking at the world through a veil of fringe is far less likely to communicate properly and make eye contact.

Stop nail biting by painting your child's nails with a foul-tasting deterrent fluid available from pharmacies. This method also cures thumb-suckers.

Don't tick them off. If your child develops a nervous tick, force yourself not to keep mentioning it to them. Rather, take steps to minimize any stresses in their life. Get up earlier in the morning to avoid a mad dash to school, stop nagging about things that don't really matter, check that they are happy with their care arrangements and, above all, make time to be calm with your child. If, despite all your efforts, the tick persists, consult your doctor.

Chapter 6
Family and friends

Parental roles

Swap jobs. Surprise your kids by sometimes doing what they expect your partner to do, so they might find one day that Daddy is doing the school run and Mummy is asking them for help to build shelves. Taking on a task that your partner usually does can make for more equitable co-parenting.

Have one-to-one time. However many kids you have, try to give each one a little time alone with you. No two family relationships are the same, so children revel in getting Mummy, Daddy or another much-loved relative all to themselves. When the family is tired and fraught, it can be helpful to split up into more manageable teams.

Have one parenting approach. If Mum is very strict and Dad very lenient, or vice versa, kids get confused and behaviour tends to suffer. Bash out your differences in private so as to be able to give your kids clear, coherent guidance.

Free your partner from parenting. Let them go on a short break with friends, take a course or just have a long lie-in occasionally. Doing things all together as a family is great, but parents need their own time for work and play.

Discuss your kids. Talk over their issues, problems – and good qualities! With an open mind, elicit your partner's advice and suggestions. Chatting over situations together will help you to respond in a reasoned, coherent way to your children's needs.

If you are really wound up about something to do with the kids, try to wait until you've talked it through together before firing on all cylinders.

Provide adjustment time. Avoid handing over the children the minute your partner comes through the front door. Allow 10 minutes' grace for them to settle back into parent mode.

Don't get personal. Arguing with your spouse or partner can sometimes be inevitable – young children can be pretty wearing – but exercise damage limitation by agreeing in advance that though you might argue over an issue, you don't trade personal insults in front of the kids.

Encourage your partner. Never vie with each other for the children's affections. Rather, observe the good things about your partner's approach to parenting, and be ready to compliment them and to boost their confidence.

Be self-aware. Imagine that you had yourself as a parent. Would you be happy? Would you like you? What would you think were your strengths and weaknesses?

Think about your friends. If you had to choose one couple to be your own parents, who would they be and why? You may be surprised by your choice, but think about it. Are you giving your child what those parents give theirs? Can you? Should you?

Separation and divorce

Explain the situation once it is a certainty – not before. Try to be clear, cool and calm, even in the face of a violent reaction from your children. If you cannot help but get upset, try to show that you are still in control. Failing that, enlist help from a close friend or family member to ensure that your children are supported as they receive the news.

Anticipate their guilt. Even if they don't articulate it, most children suspect that they are to blame for their parents' problems. Allay such fears from the outset by telling them unequivocally that it is not their fault.

Don't expect advice and support from your child. Ask for help from family and friends but avoid, if you can, burdening your child with the role of confidante and advisor.

Respect your child's love for your ex-partner. Show a decent concern for their welfare and never blacken their name to your child. If you do, it is you they will mistrust.

Play by the rules. Unless you have an overwhelming reason not to, such as real concern for your child's safety, stick to agreements you've made with your ex-partner or those agreed in court. It's tough enough for a child whose parents have separated without them being embroiled in a fight over contact. If possible, keep your child informed about the arrangements, conceal any disputes and be as dependable as possible.

Grandparents

Respect grandparent time. If your kids are happy with their grandparents, stay out of the way occasionally to give them some time to enjoy being alone together.

Remember grandparents' feelings. If they come to help you with the kids, offer them as much care and appreciation as you can.

Listen to your own parents: they did raise you! Even if many practices have changed – babies now being put to sleep on their backs, breastfeeding being recommended – this doesn't invalidate your parents' wealth of experience. Even if you don't always agree with what they say, hear them out and consider their advice.

Send school photos and copies of school reports and certificates to grandparents if they don't often see their grandchildren.

Use different names to distinguish between grandparents and avoid confusion: maternal grandparents might be Grandma and Grandpa and paternal grandparents Nan and Granddad.

Get online. If grandparents live far away, encourage them to send and receive emails, and maybe use a webcam, to stay in touch.

Encourage heart-to-hearts. If you feel that your children are bottling things up and are more likely to spill the beans to their grandparents than to you, suggest that they give them a call in privacy. You can then ask the grandparents to fill you in later!

Siblings and gender

Encourage baby love. From the birth of a new baby onwards, assume that your children love each other and want to be friends. Give older children a gift when the baby arrives, let them be involved during the early days (kids need to bond too) and show them how important they are in making their little sibling happy. Observe, praise and reward their kindnesses, and put them centre stage as the great stars of the event.

Let siblings be friends. Avoid programming your children to fall out. Comments such as "They just don't get on," "They can't help winding each other up,"or "They have nothing in common," endorse and reinforce sibling rivalries. Try to elicit warm feelings with positive comments, such as "It's unlike you two to argue," "All good friends fall out occasionally," or "You're always good at making up." Clearly you can't ignore fisticuffs, but you can play down minor disputes.

Separate rivals. Come down hard on sibling rivalry, right from the start – without getting angry. If the kids argue, just stop whatever it is they want to do and let them continue only when they have stopped arguing.

Unite your kids. Ask your jealous child whether they would really like to see their sibling fail. Explain that each member of the family contributes to the strength of the whole. Try to promote a sense of family pride in your children and teach them the importance of loyalty to each other.

Let kids raise each other. Older siblings can be as influential as parents, so let them help and advise younger ones. The advice may not always be sound – "Just hit him" is not uncommon – but is usually well meant and makes for a better sibling relationship. Don't stop younger ones from advising or comforting older siblings – they can sometimes be surprisingly wise!

Insist on civility. There's no reason why siblings shouldn't say "please" and "thank you" and show each other common courtesy. Speaking politely to each other has a remarkably civilizing effect on children's behaviour.

Offer a framework to help siblings resolve their differences, such as, "You have 20 minutes before bed, so plan how you can both have a go on the PlayStation in that time." If they can't work out their differences, separate them and stop the fun until they can.

Share and share alike. Explain that sharing makes for a bigger pool of toys, games and books than if each sibling jealously guards their own things. Equally, allow some boundaries, so that your children aren't made to share a beloved soft toy or something they've carefully constructed themselves.

Reward kindnesses between siblings with shared treats, toys or outings.

Don't favour one child over another. No parent aims to do this, but it can be difficult not to respond more positively to a compliant child than to a challenging one. Try to balance the bias by focusing on the strength of character and individuality of the less biddable child. The more calm love and attention you give them, the less they are likely to demand these responses in unacceptable ways.

Be even-handed. When tired or vexed, it can be easy to vent your frustration on the child who will take you most seriously and be most upset at your anger. If you realize that you are doing this, check yourself and dish out your chastisements fairly.

Divide your time fairly between your children. If the naughtiest child gets the most parental attention, there's a danger that the other children will emulate the behaviour so as to compete.

Believe in boys – don't stigmatize them from the start! Gender stereotyping can be just as harmful for boys as it is for girls. Remember that boys do sometimes cry, can be peaceful and quiet, can sing and dance, can work hard and conscientiously and – moreover – can be just as loving, loyal and supportive as girls.

Hold your tongue. Avoid comparisons between children, and never ask one sibling to be more like the other. When you compliment one child, try to balance it with encouragement or warm words for each of the others.

Don't let the sun go down on an argument. Try to resolve tensions and disputes before bed. Younger siblings may like to kiss each other goodnight, a little benediction that helps them drift off to sleep secure in each other's love.

Family values

Value the members of your family who love your children unconditionally. Try to welcome their advice, concern and help, even if their ideas differ markedly from your own. Kids can accommodate varying approaches, habits and attitudes more easily than we often assume.

Share your kids. The more people who care about your kids, the better. Try not to be jealous of your children's bonds with other adults. The love that they give a nanny, godparent or grandparent is not withdrawn from you, it is simply extended to them. The more people who reciprocate their love, the happier and more secure they are likely to be – and the safer. If something happened to you, they would be better off with another parental figure than without.

Arrange sleepovers with relatives before your child embarks upon sleepovers with friends. Grandparents, aunties, uncles and others are often flattered and pleased to be asked to have the children for the night. Pack some fun things (cards, board games, bouncy balls, paper and felt tips) and make sure your relative can contact you if necessary, then take the opportunity to have a night out – or in!

Allow different rules. Mum's rules will never be the same as Granny's, nor Dad's the same as his father's. Aunties and uncles will be different again. Parents can try to police the family to always impose the same rules on the kids, but are doomed to

179

failure – each adult will have their own ideas and thresholds. However, children are pretty resilient, and can adapt quickly to different "norms".

Remember to be a child. Let your kids see that you are also a child – their grandparents' child. Through your relationship with your own parents, try to demonstrate to your children filial respect, courtesy and love. If you undermine their grandparents, you'll give them the message that they may, in their turn, be disrespectful to you.

Avoid caricature. It's easy to pigeonhole kids: she's the bright one, he's the sporty one, she's the pretty one, he's the naughty one. These labels, so easily affixed, can become permanent and limiting. Parents can fail to hear the developing singing voice of a child they've called tone deaf, or the artistic talents of a mathematically gifted child.

Awaken the dead. Tell your kids about the people in your family who have died. Share stories about them, pass on their wisdoms and represent their views. Keep ancestors alive in your children's hearts and in their imaginations.

Keep family traditions alive. Pass a torch down the generations by giving your children a taste of your own childhood. You might bake a cake together using your grandmother's recipe, exhume and restore your old toys or doll's house, revisit your childhood home or simply bring out an old photo album. Show your children the evidence that you, too, were once a child.

Being a friend

Become best friends with your children (at least make this your aim!) and try to sparkle as much with them as you do with your adult friends. A firm friendship will stand you in good stead throughout the teenage years.

Broker friendships. Meeting new children can be daunting. When they are reluctant, introduce them properly, pointing out things they have in common or suggesting what they might do together – but don't force it. Let them open up in their own time.

Invite an unpopular child over to play, even if only once in a while. You may find that the child is perfectly nice and it is yours who is/are at fault, or that the children get on fine when they play together alone. If they don't, and the child proves to be a nightmare, you will at least have a clear conscience about not extending them another invitation.

Keep in touch with your child's friends from previous schools. Playing with "old friends" can be wonderfully relaxing: they are no longer in competition, playground politics are out of the way and being together recalls the sweetness of being younger.

Bridge age gaps. By fostering friendships between children of different ages. Don't restrict play dates to your children's immediate peers. There's no reason why an 8-year-old and a 12-year-old or a 10-year old and 14-year old shouldn't play happily together. The age difference can be refreshing for them all.

Defend a friend. Encourage your children to look out for their friends. Reward any care and kindness on their part, not with material things but with praise and encouragement. Kids like to make sacrifices for each other and forge official bonds of friendship, so let them!

Befriend their friends. Contrary to how it may sometimes appear, kids can be sensitive to what adults think of them. If, when little friends come to play, you are dismissive or seem uninterested in them, they'll be less likely to want to strike up a lasting friendship with your child. Rather, treat visiting kids as friends of the family and offer them no less courtesy than you extend to adult visitors.

Respect friendships between children and understand that the desire to talk about issues in their relationships may be just as pressing as your own issues. Remember that they are not yet versed in the highs and lows of human emotion, so bear with them if trivial differences assume epic proportions.

Let friends mean friends. Encourage friendships with children of both sexes, without inferring that a friend of the opposite sex is a "boyfriend" or a "girlfriend". Kids can become inhibited and wary of the opposite sex if their innocent and valuable friendships are inappropriately sexualized.

Show largesse. Even if you are not rich, you can show your children that you're prepared to be a little generous with your friends – that you can treat them to a cinema ticket or buy them a coffee, without expecting repayment!

Speak well of your friends and your children will tend to speak well of theirs.

Keep open house. Your home may be your castle, but it shouldn't become your island. Let down the drawbridge, raise the portcullis and have an informal drop-in house where people of all ages feel welcome and at ease.

Make play dates first and foremost for your kids rather than because you get on with the parents. Otherwise, sooner or later your kids will humiliate you by making it clear that they don't want to play with the hosts' children.

Tackle tensions. If your child is warring with another child, organize a play date. Get them together over something fun and distracting and give them the time and space to begin to trust each other again – though do check from time to time that they aren't beating each other up!

Have circle time. If little children are squabbling or scrapping, tell them to hold hands in a circle, then to sit down cross-legged on the floor. This basic cooperation and the unity the circle shape imposes quietens them down and makes them more biddable.

Address pseudo-sibling syndrome. If your child seems to be quarrelling constantly with a best friend, it may be that they are seeing too much of each other and starting to behave like siblings. Familiarity can breed contempt, so subtly ease off their contact until they are of a mind to miss and appreciate each other again.

Chapter 7
Emotions

Showing affection

Be physical with your kids. Kiss, cuddle, stroke and caress them. You don't need a reason to show them you love them.

Let older children into your heart – and your arms. Children, whatever their age, need affection from their parents if they are to become emotionally healthy adults. Don't smother them or insist that they reciprocate, but don't turn them away if they need safe arms around them.

Have a quiet cuddle. Kids can be consoled by explanations that help them to make sense of challenges, and comforted by words of sympathy; but sometimes words aren't enough and they need to be held, stroked, rocked and cuddled until their anguish subsides.

Chant a mantra. Distressed or over-tired children can be soothed and lulled by a simple phrase, repeated over and over: "Hush, hush, my baby ..." "Good girl ..." "Beautiful boy ...". You may well find that these little affirmations give you a lift too.

Kids aren't bed bugs! Let your children into your bed sometimes. This is where you are warm, calm and accessible, so it's not surprising that kids want to climb in for a cuddle now and again.

Share your joy with your kids. If you feel jubilant, don't hide it. Surprise your children by skipping with them down the street, singing, dancing, laughing or just showing them how wonderful you feel. Grown-ups don't always have to be grown-up!

Dealing with conflict

Don't lose it. We all blow our top sometimes, but it's not the ideal way to deal with kids. If you feel you need a deterrent to stop you from losing your cool, fine yourself. Stash the money away and, when there's enough, take your kids out for a relaxing family day together.

Offer a choice between what you would like your child to do and a less appealing option, such as going to their room. If you do this, the first option may suddenly seem more appealing!

Arguing with your partner can be unavoidable, but try not to upset your children. Shut doors so that they can't hear, and put on music or the TV to distract and soothe them. If they have to witness a row, give them the reassurance of seeing that one parent is under control and still capable of looking after them.

Promote peace. Teach your children to walk away from physical confrontations unless they have no option but to defend themselves. Sanctioning violence usually only leads to more violence.

Talk through possible solutions with your child before acting on them. Sometimes problems can evaporate just by being aired. Avoid jumping to conclusions, getting immediately on the phone or leaping to your child's defence. Hold back until all the facts are clear, you understand your child's feelings and you can do whatever's really in their best interests.

Healing wounds

Have a bag of worries. If your child is anxious or seems to be bottling something up, give them an attractive bag to put their worries in. They can write them or draw them or express them any way they choose, but once they're in the bag, they've distanced themselves from them, even if only a little. If your child is agreeable, over time you can fish the worries out one by one and talk them over together.

Hear confessions. Some children have overactive consciences and need to pour out lots of little confessions. Don't brush away these anxieties: give them your ear, but gently explain why they are not such terrible crimes as they seem. Discuss with your child the issues they raise so as to help them learn what is and isn't worth feeling guilty about.

Spill the beans. Tell your kids funny stories about your own mistakes, errors and embarrassments to help them to be less afraid of their own– and more likely to reveal them to you.

Offer charms to reassure and console your children. You could give them a dream catcher to trap nightmares, Guatemalan worry dolls to take away woes, or a perfumed handkerchief to summon the essence of someone sorely missed. Talismanic objects mean a lot to children and can help them to work through their feelings and fears.

Anticipate situations and, in simple terms, forewarn your children about things that might prove a let-down. Backup plans can help avoid massive disappointment, tears and tantrums: "If we can't get a ticket, we'll have a picnic in the garden when we go home." " If Granny isn't in, we'll go to the swings." Kids love having something – however small – to look forward to.

Plan partings. If your child has established a deep-rooted bond with a carer, be careful how you break it. If possible, phase out the care gradually over weeks or months. If it has to stop abruptly, try to maintain some contact with the carer for a while to give your child time to adjust to the separation.

If you've been ratty, tell your children that you love them before they go to bed or whisper your love to them as they sleep.

Whisper affirmations to your sleeping children. Tell them what their confidence and self-esteem need to hear: "You are beautiful." "We all love you." "Things will get better." "You are strong." "You can do it." These words may or may not infiltrate the sleeping mind, but they won't do any harm. Some children seem to sleep less fitfully after this "sleep counselling".

Gaze at your kids when they are asleep. Feast your eyes on their beautiful and peaceful faces. However tough a day you've had, this is a great reward.

Chapter 8
Behaviour

Communication

Say "please" and "thank you" to your kids and expect reciprocal politeness from them. If they are not courteous at home, they are unlikely to be courteous elsewhere.

Don't say "no" out of habit. Parents can get so used to saying "no" that they forget to listen to the question.

Make eye contact. Many parents watch their children rather than look at them. It's surprisingly easy to get out of the habit of making eye contact with our kids. Then we wonder why they don't look directly at people who talk to them!

Smile at your children when there's no reason not to. Warm parental smiles are a constant channel of love, comfort and encouragement.

Answer their questions thoughtfully and honestly. Don't ignore "silly" questions – children often have a good reason for asking them. Think what might underlie them.

Explain "why". The crude repetition of "why" is the first way in which children start trying to find out about their world. Rise to the challenge and give them a little more information with each "why" you answer.

Take note when you child says "I wish". Whether the wish is for something attainable or fanciful is an indication of your child's state of mind. Wishes can be positive or negative for kids: a great way to set goals, or a fruitless lament about what cannot be achieved or attained. Encourage your children to have good wishes, wisely wished.

First listen, then speak. Avoid telling your children what to think. Rather, discuss issues with them and listen to their views. You may find their ideas illuminating.

Have big ears for your child's worries, anxieties and obsessions. However busy you are, if there is something they need to tell you or are bursting to discuss with you, try to give them some full-on attention. Kids lay little traps to check if you are really listening, and are crushed it you aren't. Trying to understand what your children are saying to you is fundamental to good parenting, and if you can attempt to do this from when they are toddlers until they are fully grown, you won't go far wrong!

Take a child's-eye view. Avoid telling your kids that their concerns "don't matter". They matter greatly to them. Even if, from an adult perspective, the things they are concerned about seem trivial, remember they may appear insurmountable to your child.

Have a gossip. Ring-fence some chatting time when you can relax with your child and simply chew the cud. Ask them about all the latest news from school, about their friends, their hopes and concerns. Taking an interest in the things that concern them, rather than you as a parent, will help your kids realize that you do understand them and are their ally.

Make a sign that you can hold up when you are on an important call and can't be interrupted. Keep it by the phone and change it from time to time to make your kids smile. You might use a picture of their favourite celebrity with a funny speech bubble, or draw a wacky cartoon.

Teach the basics. Don't wait until your children are older to teach them how to blow their noses, eat with their mouths closed and have nice table manners. While accepting that they won't always be able to do what you ask, there's no harm in introducing these ideals to your kids when they are around three.

Learn to say "maybe". We say kids don't listen, but they rarely miss an attractive offer. Better to say "Maybe we'll go to the cinema next week", "Perhaps Granny and Grandpa can come to stay" or 'We might try that" than to present possibilities as certainties. Cancellations can be so desperately disappointing for little ones.

Use positive phrases – for example, "Give it a go!", "I bet you can!", "No problem!", "Well done!"; but don't encourage them to have unreasonable expectations by saying things such as "You can do anything!", or "You'll be the best!"

Go with it. If all the other parents have said "yes" to something, think hard before deciding you're going to be the only one to say "no". You may be right, and you may have to stick to your guns, but bear in mind that being the odd one out can be pretty traumatic for kids.

Keep secrets. If your child tells you something in confidence, keep it secret unless there's a compelling medical or safety-related reason why you should share it with a doctor or teacher. Your child should be able to tell you anything, knowing you'll respect their privacy.

Minimize lies. All parents lie occasionally, often just to keep the peace or to gloss over whatever they don't want their children to notice. Even "little white lies", though, should be used sparingly so that your kids don't start to lose trust in you.

Don't say anything that you don't want your kids to repeat!

Account for family absences in a way that your children can understand. Avoid going away without explanation as this can unsettle children far more than if they are offered a good reason for the separation: "Mummy has gone to work to get the money to pay for toys." "Daddy wants Mummy to come home again really soon, so he is going to collect her." "Grandma has gone into the hospital so that they can make her well for your birthday party!"

Keep it simple. When discussing family problems with your kids, try to avoid emotional overload. Stay calm and be honest, but spare them unnecessary detail – and unnecessary distress.

Conceal your concerns about things that your children can do nothing about. For example, if you've got a really long journey, hold back from saying "I'm worried that you children will be exhausted." As the saying goes, little pitchers have big ears, and it's not worth alarming your kids unnecessarily.

Never teach prejudice, be it about race, gender, religion, class, wealth or politics. Give your children the chance to grow up free from bigotry and able to keep their hearts and minds open to all the good things that life has to offer.

Make your own rules. Whether you are religious or not, there is no reason why you shouldn't devise a family code of conduct, either written down or simply shared and discussed with your children. Explicit moral guidelines can help kids tackle the pressures of school and the politics of friendship.

Provide food for thought. It's better to teach your children *how* to think than *what* to think. Elicit their thoughts and opinions before you offer them your own.

Don't praise everything. Kids know when your approval is automatic, and will try to catch you out. Look at what they present to you and admire what is good about it, but make some constructive suggestions about what they might try doing next time. Kids need real feedback so as to start to form their own opinions and set their own standards.

Encourage clear communication. If your children pepper their speech with filler words such as "like", "you know", "kinda", "stuff", pretend you can't quite understand them until they say what they mean clearly. Don't pull them up in this way all the time (or you'll all go mad!), only when you think these verbal ticks are really getting in the way of what they are trying to say.

Take the mickey out of your kids – not cruelly, but playfully – so that they learn to take a joke against themselves.

Explain yourself. Tell your kids why you do what you do, what your thinking is and what has shaped it. Involve your children in your decision-making, share your opinions with them and listen to theirs. From infancy to adulthood, you can talk them through issues and help them to make sense of the world through informed eyes.

Encourage vocal skills: chatting, reading aloud, singing and humming, not forgetting whooping, yodelling and whistling! Allow your children to be seen and heard.

Hear them out. Small children are often hesitant and unclear, so it can be tempting to speak for them or to interrupt a floundering explanation. Try to bite your tongue to give your kids the chance – and the time – to have their say.

Give positive attention to your kids before they provoke negative attention. Children will demand attention by being naughty if they can't get it by being good.

Discuss taboo subjects openly with your children so that they know they can always talk to you about them. If you want to broach a delicate or controversial subject, make sure that you have plenty of time to talk about it and tailor your answers to their age. **197**

Boundaries

Stay in charge. However kind, funny, relaxed and easy-going you are, remember that you are in charge of your children – not the other way round! Firm boundaries make for happier kids and, ultimately, fewer sanctions.

Have routines. Inflexible, unvarying routines can be stultifying, but children do benefit from having a basic framework for their day: if nothing else, at least regular mealtimes. If your children expect to eat a meal and do homework or chores at a certain time, they are likely to offer less resistance than if each day presents a fresh negotiation.

Just say "no". Don't be afraid of the "N" word. Kids need it sometimes. If there's something you don't want them to do, and you've good reason for not wanting them to do it, say "no" and stick to your guns. Teenagers often rely on their parents saying "no", as it helps them to resist peer pressure – they can opt out and put the blame on their parents!

"No, no, no, no, no, no ... oh all right, yes!" We all sometimes lose the will to resist pressure from our children. Better to stick to your guns, though. Try the "soft no" approach, saying each "no" more quietly and firmly. Your child will soon see that you are calm and resolute.

Aim to be consistent. It's impossible to be completely consistent, but if you tell your children off for something one day and don't the next, they won't know where they stand or what to do on the day following that. Take a look at your thresholds and try to keep them roughly in the same place.

Insist on courtesy to guests, both your guests and your child's, and on good behaviour in the presence of other people.

Don't move the goalposts when your children are aiming to reach a particular goal, or they will give up trying.

Teach children that violent behaviour – whether towards their own or the opposite sex – is wrong and won't be tolerated. The best way to prevent angry and frustrated children from becoming abusive adults is to show them how to deal positively with their negative feelings while they're still children.

Sanctions and rewards

Use a pot of pennies. Give a pot of small change to a child who is constantly misbehaving. Rather than tell them off about the same thing over and over again, simply remove a coin for every misdemeanour and put one back for every good deed. This saves you from having to lose your temper repeatedly to diminishing effect, and helps to make your rules of behaviour concrete and understandable.

Offer just desserts. Reward your children for being good, not for being naughty. When they are behaving badly, don't try to cheer them with treats, trips and toys. Rather, encourage them to earn these privileges through good behaviour: you get what you give.

Compensate your kids when they have been sorely disappointed through no fault of their own. If, for example, a friend has forgotten a play date, a longed-for event has been cancelled or they are ill and unable to go to a party, there's no harm in offering something special as a consolation prize. You might give them the chance to do something they are not usually allowed to do, spend some one-to-one time with them (doing what they enjoy) or buy a toy they've had their eye on. This isn't bribery or corruption: it's a reasonable attempt to cheer up understandably miserable kids.

Neither threaten nor offer what you can't deliver. Empty threats and idle promises erode your authority.

Use incentive schemes to tackle entrenched bad behaviour. You might instigate a reward chart with stars or stickers, but avoid awarding "black" or negative marks.

Have a target box. Agree a target or goal with your child. It might be something like, "I will not cry when Daddy drops me at playgroup" or "I will be nice to my baby brother." Write the target down on a piece of paper and put it in a special box. Tell your child that when the target is achieved, the paper will be replaced with a coin, a sweet or whatever you think will be a good incentive.

Warn before you punish. Children should always be given the chance to reform! Warnings need to be calm, simple and audible if they are to be effective.

Put yourself in their shoes. Imagine that you are on the receiving end of the sort of reprimands you give your children. Would they seem fair and persuasive or frightening and immoderate? Take a clear-eyed look at how you handle your anger, and adjust your approach if you don't like what you see.

Stick to the point. Tell your children off clearly and specifically for whatever they have done wrong – and don't spuriously attack things they hold dear. So, for example, you might say "I've asked you twice not to pick your nose and will be angry if you do it again," but should avoid, "Do you learn so little in that school of yours that you and your friends can't even blow your own noses?"

Think before you speak and speak before you smack, then there's a chance you can avoid smacking your child. Make some rules: never smack hard, never smack in anger – ideally, never smack at all.

Have a naughty chair or stair to which your children can be sent if they've overstepped the mark. Five minutes is enough for a small child (don't keep any child there for long periods of time). It's a good alternative to smacking, giving everyone a bit of time out in which to calm down. Where behaviour is very bad, as a last resort you may need to use a "naughty room", but first be absolutely sure that all hazards are removed and it is completely safe for them to be alone in it.

Punish the wrongdoer, not the whole family.

Never withdraw your love by way of punishment. It's too cruel and offers children nothing to be good for. Make it clear to your kids that now and forever they have your unconditional love, whether they succeed or fail, please or displease you.

Responsibility and independence

Give them what you want. If you want your children to act responsibly, give them some responsibilities.

Don't do everything for your kids. It can seem easier and quicker to clean, tidy and organize them, but in the long term it will lead to more work for you. Even toddlers enjoy small responsibilities, such as putting a toy away or clearing their plate from the table. Chores and obligations shouldn't dominate young lives, but children like to do some things for themselves.

Skivvy not! Don't run unnecessary errands. If your children are always asking you for things they can easily get for themselves, politely suggest that they use their own legs.

Empower children by letting them do things not just for themselves, but for each other. If your child can perfectly well put out drinks for friends, or take people's coats, or get breakfast for a sibling, don't take over.

Offer choices between options that are acceptable to you. That way, everyone is happy!

Let them find their feet without telling them that they might stumble. Children are very suggestible and will curb their aspirations if you are too quick to question their abilities.

Actions not words. Explain that the word "sorry" is useful only if it means, "I will try not to do it again", and that all apologies are only as good as the actions that follow them.

Combat disaffection with involvement. Children of all ages are generally more contented once they have a role. Whether it's washing up, gardening, making something, decorating or sewing, give your child a task that is achievable and rewarding.

Work animal magic by giving your child their own pet to look after. Knowing that the animal is solely dependent on them can give them a first taste of real responsibility.

Teach them to live by their own lights, not to be led astray by other people's.

Take the long view. Separation can be as upsetting for parents as it is for some children. If you're dreading the school trip and think you'll be anxious the whole time your child is away, remember that in all likelihood it will be a great experience from which they'll grow in confidence and independence. A little time apart from parents (with all their concerns) can be truly liberating for a child.

Ward off homesickness with a few well-chosen words prior to your child's departure: "If you feel upset, it will only be because you are tired, so try to have a good rest and you'll feel a lot better in the morning." "I've put a kiss on Teddy's nose, so there's always a kiss there from me, if you want one." "If any of your friends feel homesick, you can comfort them." Tread carefully, so as to strike a balance between equipping your child with coping strategies and over-sensitizing them to the possibility of homesickness.

Beware of phone calls just before bedtime. When you are separated from your child, it seems natural to call and say goodnight before they go to bed. One imagines that it will help them to sleep, and for some children it does. For others, however, it serves as a shocking reminder of your absence and brings on a great rush of emotion. If your child is prone to homesickness, it can be best to phone sometime during the day, when they are rested and busy doing something interesting.

See into the future. New experiences, even pleasant ones, can shock or overawe a child. As far as is possible, prepare your child in advance for what they haven't encountered before: "You might not be able to see Mummy from the stage, but I'll be there." "The doctor will need you to open your mouth like a tiger." "If you wake up in the night-time and want Mummy, Teddy will comfort you." Kids can benefit from being equipped with coping strategies in advance.

Spread their wings. Within the bounds of good sense and safety, allow your kids to attempt things, even if they seem beyond their capabilities. Far from putting them off, failure may prove the spur to success – and by starting young, they may attain excellence sooner than most. If not, encourage them to try again, maybe when they are a little older!

Respect and courtesy

Have a light heart and a light touch, and your kids will too. Their behaviour starts with yours, so calmly ask your child to calm down and politely ask your child to be polite. Set an example that isn't a mixed message.

Don't engage with a child who is being unreasonable. If they say something such as, "I hate you," don't follow up either by retaliating or by asking why. Rather, tell the child clearly what the sanction will be if such behaviour is repeated.

Appeal to your child's goodwill. Kids enjoy pleasing their parents, so instead of "Don't you dare ...", try "It would be great if you could avoid ...", "I'd be really pleased if you'd try not to ..." or "I'm sure you know not to ...".

Avoid pet names. Strike a deal: if you don't embarass your children by calling them by their pet names in public or when their friends visit, they will allow you to use – and enjoy – the names in private!

Introduce your children to people they haven't met before, just as you would with an adult.

Point out role models. Tell your children about the people – alive or dead – whom you respect most. Explain to your kids what their values and achievements mean and how they have affected the lives of others.

Offer some guidance. Morality isn't inborn: children have to learn it, which can be a painful process. From early on give them some help by explaining, as simply as possible, the basics: don't try to upset or hurt people on purpose, and tell a grown-up immediately if someone is upsetting or hurting you.

Foster a sense of community, and the reciprocation that this entails. If a friend or neighbour has been particularly kind to your child, encourage them to repay the kindness by doing an errand for them, making them a card or giving them a little gift.

Nurture empathy. Discuss other people's situations with your kids and encourage them to imagine how other people feel.

Question your own authority. Are your parental decisions sound and consistent? Or are they arbitrary? For example, why do you agree to X but not to Y? Why shouldn't your child do Z? On reflection, you may think that your decisions are fine; or you may realize that you need to rationalize them.

Chapter 9
Wisdom

Doing your best

Love your children unconditionally, just as your children will love you whatever you say or do. Cherish this love and never betray it.

Break negative cycles. We all get into habits, but sometimes we need to take a look at the way we do things and think how we might adapt and change. Do your kids push the same buttons over and over again? How can you break a cycle of provocation and retaliation? You might try not taking the bait, removing the trigger of conflict or giving your child more attention when you are calm and relaxed.

Use your power over your children to be constructive and fair. To your children you reign supreme, so be careful never to toy or trifle with their affections, and certainly don't take out your frustrations on them just because you can.

Apologize to your children if you are in the wrong. There's no danger in being honest: it will teach them to be as open as you are.

Cry, if you must. You don't always have to hide your emotions from your children, but try not to dramatize situations or to turn on tears to win their compliance.

Show self-control. All parents get grumpy sometimes, but try not to be tactless or hurtful to your kids when you are feeling short-tempered. If you can avoid saying things you'll regret, you'll all feel fine when the gloom lifts.

Don't tread on dreams. Children are always hatching plans – some more convenient than others! If you are not keen that they should rearrange all the furniture, paint a mural on the wall, make their own frame for your most cherished photograph or any other such scheme, let them down gently. Imagine how you would feel if someone stopped you from achieving your goals, and look for ways of channelling the enterprise rather than crushing it.

Be amazed. Try to avoid giving your children the impression that you have been everywhere and done everything before them. Whenever possible, allow them to unfold some new experiences for you.

Watch your kids when they're not aware that you can see them. If possible, observe them as they interact with others. How happy do they seem with other children or with carers? Is their behaviour surprising to you? Are you taken aback by their independence? Try to be realistic in your assessment of how they seem to be faring – and try to learn from what you see.

Account for yourself. If for any reason you are acting differently from normal, let your children know how you are feeling. Even if you aren't able to tell them why you feel as you do, they'll be reassured to know that there's a reason for your change of mood.

Do it now, if "it" is playing with your children, reading them a bedtime story and giving them a reassuring cuddle. Do it later, if "it" is tidying up or chatting on the phone to friends when your children need your attention.

Set an example, even when you fail to set an example! Explain why you shouldn't have done what you've done, and let them know how you intend to put things right or make amends.

Spread a little happiness. If you do a little good for other people whenever you can, your children are likely to pick up the habit of trying to make things better, not worse!

Teach mind over matter. Don't talk about money more than necessary. If their parents' conversation revolves around finance, purchases and prices, kids will follow suit. Encourage your children to appreciate the value and meaning of things before they are aware of the cost.

Seek out ethical products. Children – particularly babies – can be environmentally unfriendly. Check on the Internet for ethical products and services that benefit the planet and your child's health. Ordinary disposable nappies can contain artificial chemical absorbents such as sodium polyacrylate, but it is possible to source alternatives that are free of this and of perfume, dye and latex. Terry nappies, too, which are undergoing something of a revival, offer a good alternative because they can be reused.

Ask questions, take up opportunities, follow whims and show your children – by example – how to take initiatives.

Don't spoon-feed your kids. If they want something in a shop or a restaurant, encourage them to ask for it themselves. If they've lost something, let them look for it and try to work

out how they might find it. It can seem like kindness to steer your
children through every situation, but whenever possible,
let them handle things themselves.

Share your talents. Whatever you are good at, share with
your children. Avoid the "I did this but wouldn't recommend it to
you" attitude that prevents so many parents from passing on their
skills. Children are discriminating: they pick and choose from our
traits and talents. Often they improve on what we can give them,
fashioning out of our enthusiasms their own future successes.

Remember the things you loved as a child, and try to give
your children the chance of having the same fun. Were you mad
about a musical box, your stamp collection, a tree house, Punch
and Judy shows, the smell of freshly baked bread or toasting
marshmallows on the fire? Give, show or demonstrate to your
children the things that were precious to you, but don't be
disappointed if they turn out to have quite different tastes
and interests.

Don't chuck out things that are of emotional value to your
children without first checking with them. Be careful, too, not
to abandon or throw away any token that they have given to
you. Kids can be deeply offended to find their labour of love
consigned to the bin, but delighted to find it promoted to
the mantelpiece.

Hang on to their youth! Childhood isn't just a rehearsal for
adulthood, so try not to turn your child's early years into a race

to grow up. Childhood is possibly the most precious period of life, when the days can seem endless, pleasures intense and new experiences utterly captivating.

Look after yourself so that you can look after your children. There is no excuse for trashing your body if your children are reliant upon you. If you smoke, face up to the fact that you risk not seeing your kids grow up. Giving up is hard, but so is dying.

Get well. If you are suffering psychologically or physically, seek help. Don't wait until you are seriously depressed or in pain. As a parent you are a front-line key worker, so take your own needs seriously and address them promptly.

Give them a rock. Kids need to feel that they have at least one rock – a person whom they can rely upon totally and trust unquestioningly. If for any reason or at any time you can't be that rock, call in someone else – maybe a grandparent, a godparent or a good friend – to offer the comfort and security they need.

Believe in yourself. If you think that your child really needs you, if you suspect that they are sickening for something, if you feel that they are hiding something or have something on their mind, trust and act on your intuition.

Silently renew your vows to your children throughout their childhood and beyond: "I will love you and care for you and do the very best for you, from this day forward, forever more."

Acceptance

Don't be alarmed. We all worry about our children and live in fear that something untoward may happen to them. All we can actively do is exercise due caution and care. Ironically, if we cocoon our kids and posit danger all around – "You will fall", "You will get ill" – we can inhibit their ability to handle dangerous situations safely. We need to strike a balance between recklessness and over-caution.

Don't panic. In a few years your child is unlikely still to be having tantrums, wetting the bed, crying when you leave the room or sucking their thumb. All these phases soon pass. When a current problem is plaguing you, think of how a previous one has evaporated.

Have realistic goals. Children who are constantly striving to meet impossible targets will always feel like failures, however clever or talented they may be. Encourage your kids to aim a little higher, but not above their reach or capacity. Do you do ballet, play the cello, speak three languages and excel at sport?

Lighten the load. Make sure that your children realize your affection is not dependent on their success and that they don't think that your reputation depends on their achievements.

Go with the grain. Recognize and respect your children's likes, dislikes and abilities, even if they are in areas that have previously been of little interest to you. Allow your kids to introduce you to new ideas and experiences. Not only will you then start to appreciate what makes them tick, you may also get real pleasure from the things they enjoy.

Respect repetition. Kids love to reread books and to watch the same movies and cartoons over and over again. Strange as this may seem to adults, it is common childhood behaviour. Without thwarting the instinct to revisit whatever is adored, try subtly to introduce new material when you feel they are ready for something more stimulating.

Call it a day. If your child is frightened by a movie or something on TV, be prepared to walk out or switch off. Kids should be allowed to decide for themselves what they can and can't handle. Be highly cautious about letting them view movies or use games intended for older children or adults. Little kids are far more likely to confuse fiction with reality and to try to emulate what they see on the screen.

Relax the dress code. Kids aren't dolls; we can't dress them up forever. By the age of seven most have developed distinct tastes and preferences. You may not particularly like or approve of their style but, so long as they are warm and dry, does it really matter? Strike a bargain: if you don't interfere most of the time, they'll agree to dress the part once in a while when it's important.

Allow sadness. Just like adults, kids aren't always happy. Accept that your children may sometimes feel a bit blue, and allow them the time and space to express what is, after all, a normal human emotion.

Quit worrying. Recognize that most families go through tough patches, where everyone seems out of sorts and parents wonder if they have "failed" in the great task of bringing up their kids. More often than not, these phases pass and are forgotten – children bounce back to normal and parents' spirits revive.

If they are driving you crazy, pause and think how you would feel if they couldn't.

Accept difference. Few kids are entirely "normal": they all have their quirks and foibles. Cherish your children as much for their particularity as for their normality.

Be flexible. As a parent, you have to make plans, but you also have to be prepared for them to change – or fall apart totally! Illness, other children's illnesses, kids changing their minds and deciding they don't after all want to do what they thought they wanted to do – all these situations inevitably challenge the best-laid schemes. Rather than getting stressed and guilt-tripping those who have caused the change of plan, try to be calm and magnanimous. There's usually nothing you can do about the situation, so you may as well accept it with good grace!

Share your plans. Your children may not always want to do what you want them to do. Rather than drag them along reluctantly, try to involve them in your plans, giving them a sense of the timing, sequence and purpose of what is to be done. If they feel that they have been involved and consulted, they may be more willing to participate.

Celebrate hard-won achievements. If your child is among the last to learn to speak, walk, read or ride a bike, there's all the more reason to celebrate their achievement when it happens.

Focus on your own child's results. Avoid making your children compare themselves with others. Tempting as it is, resist the desire to ask your kids' about their classmates' grades and results.

Demonstrate tolerance. Most of us have pet hates, things that really wind us up: noisy neighbours, other people's personal habits, unruly dogs. Rather than pass on these sensitivities to our children, it's best to keep quiet about them in the hope that our kids may not inherit a lifetime of irritation.

Check your blind spot. All parents have a blind spot. It might be allowing their kids to interrupt, not insisting on a decent bedtime or failing to introduce their children to a wide enough variety of foods. Whatever it is, it is not the be all and end all, so avoid taking offence if a well-meaning relative or friend points it out!

Smile! When everything seems to have gone wrong – if, for example, your children are up late, arguing, not yet fed and the place is a tip – there's no point in freaking out. Try to see the funny side of the situation, and salvage it with good grace.

Going with the flow

Don't be taken in by the perfect mothers and babies on food packaging and in baby magazines. Having babies is a mucky, tiring, scary endurance test, but all the more wonderful for being a real experience, not an ersatz marketing mirage.

Banish snobbery. There's no place for it when raising children. Whatever your pet hate – be it Barbie, pink plastic ponies, trading cards, combat trousers, huge trainers or spiky haircuts – they're not worth getting steamed up about. Having happy, healthy kids is all that really matters.

Use avoidance tactics. If you are frayed, frazzled or just not coping well, hold back from losing control. Pause – even if for only a few seconds – and think about what you can best do to avoid meltdown. Phone a friend for a chat, put the children in front of a favourite video or give them a treat to lighten everyone's mood. If you feel you are at breaking point, don't be afraid to drop your standards for a moment rather than do or say something you'll regret.

Let them grow. If your child feels ready to take a new step, don't automatically stop them out of fear or habit. Look at it from their point of view. Is it important to them? Is there any real harm in it? Why shouldn't they? If you still think that it's too early for them or that they aren't yet ready, at least you'll have thought through the issues and won't be making arbitrary decisions.

Live large. If you focus on living rather than just achieving, you'll never have the chilling realization that you've missed enjoying your kids grow up.

Be mischievous. Why shouldn't you be a bit eccentric sometimes, even if you embarrass your children in the process? It's better to be a nutty parent than a stressed one!

Wear bright clothes. For days spent with your kids, ditch the adult uniform of greys, browns and blacks. Cheer up your wardrobe with some casual clothes in a palette of your children's favourite colours.

Debunk the things that frighten your kids: "That spider couldn't even eat an flea!" "The baddy's fangs are plastic pretend ones." Or, if you are absolutely sure your child won't quote you, "If the angry teacher scares you, imagine her sitting on the loo!"

Let it pass. Allow the grudges and frustrations of family life to run through your fingers like sand. If you argued with your family in the morning, don't nurse your wrath all day so that the disagreement is resumed as soon as everyone comes home. Just let the anger drain away so that you can start afresh when you regroup.

Peace of mind

Deflect anger with humour. Children love a giggle and are more easily diffused by a joke than a rebuke. Trying to make a sulky child smile is less of a challenge than it seems. See if you can tickle their funny bone and get a laugh.

Convert negative energy into positive. Advise your children to use their anger rather than be taken over by it. When you or they have a problem, sit down and make an action plan. Anger can be a great catalyst and driver.

Don't shoot the messenger! Hold your tongue about problems that are not of your child's making. It's not your child's fault if the school bus was late arriving at school, if the teacher hasn't returned a book needed for homework or if a friend spoils something they have been kind enough to lend them. When you are given irritating news, pause to consider whether your child is really to blame.

Don't catastrophize! Avoid making a big deal out of something that isn't very important, otherwise your child may find it difficult to work out what really matters. Bear in mind how easily alarmed small children can be. If you say that it's the end of the world, they'll believe it is.

Don't guilt-trip your kids. If your child has been in the wrong but has tried to put things right and has said sorry, there's little point in continuing to be angry with them. Constant references to previous misdemeanours can undermine a child's confidence and dent their sense of self-worth.

Grant their freedom. Explain to your kids that the one place they can be free is in their own minds. Nobody else is privy to their thoughts, and no one can police them. This can be a very comforting idea for older children wrestling with the restrictions of home, school and circumstance.

Why beat yourself up? Parenting is a 24/7 job: you're not going to do it perfectly all the time, so let yourself off the hook for minor mistakes. Don't dwell on them. Instead, put your energies into doing your best in the here and now.

Think big. Save your worrying and concern for the things that really matter.

Lighten up. If you are feeling blue, try to remember that being a parent is a wonderful gift, which is not granted to everyone.

Stay on an even keel. Mood swings can be very unsettling for kids. Most parents have them (it's a stressful job!), but it's worth checking on yourself from time to time to make sure that you aren't taking out on your children frustrations that have nothing to do with them.

Be kind. Every parent is different and there is no one formula for parenting, but if you are kind to your kids and what you do is motivated by kindness, you can't go that far wrong.

Point out the good more often than the bad – in your children, in other people and in the world.

Be still. If you feel that your children are stressed, anxious or over-tired, encourage stillness in your home. Set an example by settling down with a book or doing something quiet and contemplative. Parents set the pace, which sometimes should be slow!

Breathe yourself calm. If you are tired but can't have any time out, take a few long, deep breaths to calm and energize yourself. Exhale slowly through your mouth, imagining that you are blowing the stress out of your body and mind.

Always a parent

Let yourself be overwhelmed by the sheer miracle of having made your children. While watching them with their friends, absorbed in a task or fast asleep, take time just to feel the wonder of being a parent.

Abandon objectivity. You should always be biased towards your children. It is a pillar of unconditional love. If you think that they are the loveliest, cleverest, most beautiful, generous and entertaining people in the world, they are – just as in their eyes, you are the best parents in the world!

Posit a bright future for your kids that they can aspire to and work towards.

Tell them! Don't keep it a secret from your kids that you love and adore them and always will. And if you have a lovely, complimentary thought about them, there's no reason not to share it with them.

Boast about your children to your family, but spare your friends (especially those with kids).

Make a will. From the day you become parents, you should have wills that clearly state what you want to happen to your offspring in the event of your dying – who should look after them and how they should be provided for. Take out insurance, if affordable, to cover the cost of raising your kids, and draft up wills with a good, reputable solicitor, whom you can rely on to have the children's best interests at heart. You might also consider writing private letters to your children, which can be lodged with the solicitor and held alongside the wills.

Send good vibes to your children when you are apart. Think of what they might be doing and send your love out to them. If they are facing a challenge and you can't be with them, watch the clock and, at the appropriate time, focus all your energy on them.

Stand back, smile and let your kids get on with inheriting the world.

Index

Author's Acknowledgments

I am extremely grateful for the ideas and advice offered by the following people: Philippa Browne, Julia Challender, Ingrid Court-Jones, Alro Craig, Kevin Douglas, Miriam Grabiner, Susan and Roland Green, Paul Greenwood, Melissa Greenwood, Melanie Harris, Rohina Ilyas, John Isbister, Biba Kang, Sky Kang, Dharminder Kang, Michelle Lewis, Carol Lloyd-Morris, Melissa Malcolm and Sasha Delve, Sybil Mercer, Miranda Newsom, Claire Nielson, Adam Parfitt, Jane Rogoyska, Harb and Dalou Sangha, Bob Saxton, Shane and Janet Sayers, Philip, Mina and James Thompson, Joanna Wormald; parents at University College School, Hampstead, London; parents at Haberdashers' Aske's School for Girls, Elstree, Hertfordshire; and parents far and wide!

Emergency/useful numbers

Doctor:

Emergency Doctor:

Paediatrician:

Dentist:

Emergency Dentist:

Pharmacy:

Optician:

Useful organisations and helplines: